Image of Excellence

Wisdom and Inspiration
for Today's Businesswoman

Image of Excellence

Wisdom and Inspiration for Today's Businesswoman

By
Valerie Grant-Sokolosky

Tulsa, Oklahoma

Image of Excellence —
Widsom and Inspiration
for Today's Businesswoman
ISBN 1-56292-078-2
P. O. Box 55388
Tulsa, Oklahoma 74155-1388

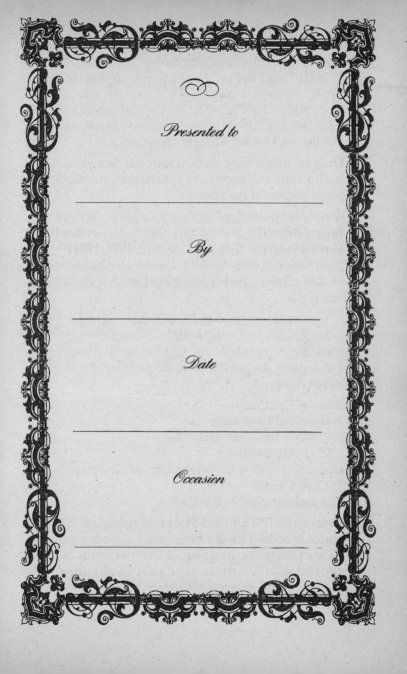

Presented to

_____

By

_____

Date

_____

Occasion

_____

CONTENTS

Part VI — 31-Day Devotional
By John Mason

THE VIRTUOUS WOMAN

A wife of noble character who can find? She is worth far more than rubies.

Her husband has full confidence in her and lacks nothing of value.

She brings him good, not harm, all the days of her life.

She selects wool and flax and works with eager hands.

She is like the merchant ships, bringing her food from afar.

She gets up while it is still dark; she provides food for her family and portions for her servant girls.

She considers a field and buys it; out of her earnings she plants a vineyard.

She sets about her work vigorously; her arms are strong for her tasks.

She sees that her trading is profitable, and her lamp does not go out at night.

In her hand she holds the distaff and grasps the spindle with her fingers.

She opens her arms to the poor and extends her hands to the needy.

When it snows, she has no fear for her household; for all of them are clothed in scarlet.

She makes coverings for her bed; she is clothed in fine linen and purple.

Her husband is respected at the city gate, where he takes his seat among the elders of the land.

She makes linen garments and sells them, and supplies the merchants with sashes.

She is clothed with strength and dignity; she can laugh at the days to come.

She speaks with wisdom, and faithful instruction is on her tongue.

She watches over the affairs of her household and does not eat the bread of idleness.

Her children arise and call her blessed; her husband also, and he praises her:

"Many women do noble things, but you surpass them all."

Charm is deceptive, and beauty is fleeting; but a woman who fears the LORD is to be praised.

Give her the reward she has earned, and let her works bring her praise at the city gate.

Proverbs 31:10-31

P A R T   I

MOTIVATION:

Improving Your Self-Image

By
Valerie Grant-Sokolosky

"If you shoot for the moon,
you'll always land among the stars."

Valerie Grant-Sokolosky

CHAPTER 1

GO FOR IT!

Go for it! How often people who love and believe in me have encouraged me with those words. It wasn't always easy to put forth the effort to achieve success — to keep on keeping on. Hurts and disappointments have hit me, but nothing kept me from keeping on, even when there didn't seem to be any reason to continue.

Success may elude you for a season, a day, or a year, but then the right time comes when all of the circumstances seem to fall perfectly together. Adversity comes to everyone. You don't have to anticipate it or put it on your calendar. It will find you. The critical factor is how you respond to it when it hits.

My story is not one of continuous success, but one of many, many failures mixed with moments of success. We rarely read or hear that most winners fail much more often than they experience success. How can you spot a winner? She's the one who picks herself up and keeps going.

Two years ago I put together a television show on fashion tips. I took the idea to three stations. Two of the stations seemed interested and even allowed me to do a few shows, only to say later that they didn't have the budget to continue. I pursued my idea and then got a lucky break. No, not blind luck, but luck defined as preparedness meeting opportunity, mixed with faith.

A television station contacted me. They needed someone to do a fashions tips segment. I had already done several pilots for the other stations and was ready. I got the show!

A friend of mine enjoys putting together collages. She tells me that when all the pieces are cut out and strewn over the floor, there seems to be no possibility that they could ever fit together. Yet when the final picture is completed, a lovely scene is formed.

Life is learning to fit. In building a wardrobe you can combine an inexpensive item with the proper accessories to create an expensive-looking outfit. It's a matter of appropriately fitting the clothes and proper accessories together which makes the outfit work.

We need to fine tune ourselves to success — to make the right selections and to focus our direction on excellence. Be prepared when the opportunities open. Be ready for your season of success.

The Right Season: The Time Is Now!

What? *Me* start a new career after twenty years of devoting myself to being a wife and mother? *Me* step into a new career at the age of thirty-nine? It just can't be done. Especially not in the fashion-conscious city of Dallas. How could I make an impact in the field of fashion when so many long-time professionals have already made their mark for so many years?

For fourteen years I encased my life with raising my three precious children — changing diapers, going to PTA meetings, driving in carpools, cooking, and keeping a household intact. I was completely dedicated to this life and, more importantly, I loved it! My husband had been busy making his mark in the business world. The thought of returning to a career had not even entered my mind until I found myself with a strange yearning to do something again in the fashion world. The children were older, no longer needing the bedtime tuck-ins and constant watching over. They had grown into three healthy, active teenagers who were no longer dependent on me. Their lives were filled with activities and friends.

"Lord, this just isn't right," I reasoned. "I'm not supposed to have a career as long as the children are home." I really felt guilty even thinking of working. "Lord, You've blessed me with such a lovely family; I should be completely content just meeting their needs. I've already had a glamorous career early in life. Please! If this desire for a career is not from You, and I can't imagine that it is, just take the desire away."

The desire didn't leave. The yearning deep in my heart kept growing. Summer was approaching, and I had been invited to the Oregon coast. My husband was completely involved with his work. The children and I could visit the seashore and get away from the usual routine. This might be a good time to think things through clearly, get my head on straight, and realize this yearning of mine was just a fantasy. "Great," I decided. "We'll go!"

Excitedly, my two boys and daughter anticipated fun at the beach. We were eager for a solid rest and a time of relaxation. I was especially looking forward to having some quiet time, walking along the beach and talking to God. I hoped He would resound some wonderful wisdom right out of the waves.

While we were planning for our trip, a dear and discerning friend visiting me made this statement: "Valerie, I have just the thing for you!" She began sharing about a new career field called *image development.* "It's related to things you've done in the past, and it's a business all your own, something you can do part-time or however often you want."

It sounded wonderful.

In Oregon I casually went into a bookstore and selected a book on color analysis. I started reading. Fascinated, I couldn't put it down. It described how to match your personal coloring of hair, skin, and eyes with complementary colors in your wardrobe to create a harmonious visual impact.

But I quickly became frustrated. The color analysis system presented exciting possibilities, but it also left me confused. It was categorized into four seasons. I was able to place myself in every one.

"I must be a woman for all seasons," I decided. "Am I a summer or a winter?" Some of the colors in each category seemed to look exactly right. As I became more frustrated with my lack of understanding, the desire to be trained in the color analysis business began to grow. Somehow I knew this training would be the beginning of my return into the image and personal development field.

When I returned home from my vacation, I discussed everything with my husband. He encouraged me, and I began looking for companies where I could receive training. Some of the companies I found were far away and some very expensive.

One day, a phone call came from a woman I didn't even know. She said, "I understand you are looking into color-analysis training. I'm attending a meeting being held by a company who does training in this field. Would you like to go with me?"

I almost fell out of my chair. "Of course," I said.

That was my answer to prayer. I said, "Thanks, God! That's just like You to work that way."

I became certified in color analysis. Soon after I began studying this field, I realized why I hadn't been able to figure out which "season" I was. Although the book I had read during my vacation had been instrumental in whetting my appetite for more knowledge, it had not included all the necessary information. I became exuberant, excited about the field I had always loved: clothing and fashion. I'd always enjoyed helping people look their best, and teaching image development gave me great fulfillment.

As I prepared to start my business, I questioned the Lord, "Where will I find clients?" I knew I couldn't pull people in from the street. "I know," I thought. "I'll begin with my friends." And I did.

As the weeks and months passed, I became absolutely engrossed with this new opportunity. I started advertising and calling the newspapers to let them know what I was doing. I was excited about image development and shared with everyone how newsworthy I thought the field was.

Image development and color analysis were taking the country by storm. To my amazement my business began getting publicity. The first was a full-page article with a color picture in the fashion segment of the major Dallas paper!

Unbelievable! I thought. Yet I knew that all things are possible through God.

Then came an article about wardrobe consulting in *D Magazine*, one of the most highly respected magazines in Dallas. Next, a newspaper did a series of articles on image. Television opportunities on three of the local networks developed, with the programs "Your Best Colors" and "Your Image."

My husband was jogging one evening near our home when a neighbor stopped him. "Doug," he said, "I've certainly seen your wife's picture and articles about her in the papers a lot lately. Who is her P.R. agent?"

Doug laughed. We both knew that I have the best public relations agent there is — God. When He's for you, who can be against you??

As the years passed, my business grew. More and more people were becoming aware that this information would aid them in becoming all they can be and developing all that God has given them. It's never too late. God's timing is always perfect. He can do all things if we will only trust Him.

What is your dream? What is your heart's desire? What do you want to learn or achieve? Remember the definition of luck: preparedness meeting opportunity, mixed with faith.

Be prepared for your opportunities. My story is not unusual or similar success for you impossible. Success is attainable by anyone. The ingredients are the same: Decide what you want to do, set a goal for your career, and gain the knowledge or training you need to achieve your goal. Then *go for it*! Opportunities will come to you as you pursue your goal with a positive outlook and determination.

A friend recently asked me, "What is it that makes you strive so hard to achieve?"

I answered, "I never set goals that are unattainable, and I always intend to succeed."

Never give up: don't let setbacks stop you. When adversity comes, remember: it may knock you down, but it can't keep you down unless you allow it. Your season of success is predictable when you know God is for you, and you refuse to give up.

CHAPTER 2

EXERCISES FOR EXCELLENCE

Here are some exercises that will help you create your image of excellence and begin to establish an atmosphere of success in your life.

Imagine Yourself Successful

Always picture yourself successful. See the new you whom you desire to become. Set aside time each day to be alone and undisturbed. Get comfortable and relax completely. Close your eyes and reflect on where you are now and where you want to be in the future. See yourself in your new career, capable, and full of self-confidence. Imagine every detail, and capture that picture in your mind. When discouragements come throughout the day, pull that image up in your mind and look at it.

Remember Your Past Successes

Rehearse your past successes. Never minimize any success you have experienced, no matter how small that success may seem. Write down your successes. You will be surprised how much a well-kept diary will encourage you when things don't seem to be going your way. Look back and remember your successes. Develop the habit of focusing your attention on these. Everything we do in life can become a habit, either good or bad. Maintaining a habit of focusing on the positive somehow generates even more positive experiences.

Forget the Failures

What do we do with the failures? They are real, too. If we're smart and care about our own well-being, we'll learn from the failures, then *forget them*. Dwelling on past failures causes "loser's syndrome."

Instead, pick yourself up, dust yourself off, and keep striving for that *image of excellence*. Just as there are seasons of success, there are also times when failure can be caused by wrong timing and uncontrollable circumstances. Take responsibility for your life, but not for the failures. Learn from them, but don't be overcome by them.

Celebrate Your Successes

No matter how minor they may seem to be, celebrate your successes! They need to be celebrated. Your successes are your memory makers.

When your child comes home with a good grade, celebrate it. When you make that sale, take the family to dinner. When your husband is promoted, buy a meaningful card and use candles on the table. Think of ways that are your very own. Each celebration will make a marker for remembering your successes.

Not long ago my family seemed to hit nothing but brick walls. It was happening to each one of us; my husband, my children, and me. Projects we tried to develop couldn't get off the ground. Sales we needed to generate weren't coming in. Opportunities seemed far away, and doors always closed to us. Finally, we sat down together and discussed the situation. We all agreed that we appeared to be completely surrounded by brick walls. But as we talked through this, we realized we had to make a decision. The choice was ours. We could either give up or keep on. Because our habit of keeping on and encouraging one another was established, the choice was made.

The past successes were there telling us, "You've made it in the past, you can do it again." We decided to shoot for the moon and believe we would at least land among the stars. Not long after we made this definite decision, opportunities opened and the seasons of success began again. We celebrated each success as it came.

Set Definite Goals

Nothing happens by accident. Opportunities come, but you would never be ready for them if you didn't have a clear direction and already knew where you wanted to go. Setting goals *does* make the difference.

From the beginning of our marriage, my husband and I have set goals. While the children were still young, we started including them in a goal-setting exercise we do at least once a year.

On New Year's Eve, we celebrate together and reflect on what has happened during the past year. Then we dream, hope, and plan for the next year. Each of us writes on a piece of paper three definite, attainable goals for our mental, spiritual, and physical life. I put these in an envelope and seal it. On the following New Year's Eve we open the envelope. It's exciting and fun to see if the goals have been fulfilled.

Respond Positively to Life

This final exercise is for developing a positive self-image and response to life. Each of us has an image of ourself that is the result of unconscious reactions to past experiences, successes, or failures. Our minds are like sensitive computers. What we put into our computer determines our future response to life.

I have a friend who remembers rainy days as wonderful moments in her childhood. Her mother baked goodies on those days. When my friend came home from school, she smelled the sweet aroma of a freshly baked pie or cake. She does the same for her family. To this day she loves what to me are dreary, rainy days.

I always disliked rainy days, because I couldn't go out and play. I was an only child and wanted to be around other children all the time. I'm still a people person. My computer was programmed negatively about rainy days. I can now change my response because I have insight.

There are so many things in this world which are completely beyond your control. But your image, your positive reactions to life, and your decisions are completely within your control. Change the input and thus control the output.

"Part I" is from *Seasons of Success* by Valerie Grant-Sokolosky (Tulsa: Honor Books, 1985), pp. 15-22, 25-28.

PART II

PROTOCOL IN BUSINESS

By
Valerie Grant-Sokolosky

CHAPTER 3

RELATIONSHIPS
IN BUSINESS

Today one of the most common concerns among men is, "How am I supposed to treat a woman who is now my business equal?" and for women, "Should I expect the traditional female courtesies when I am an executive?"

Because women have been achieving high levels of success, the role of the female has changed. No longer is she employed only as a secretary, but also as a boss and peer. This puts a whole new code of conduct into effect among the office staff as to how to treat women in the day-to-day activities at work.

You as a woman can and should set the stage for how you *want* to be treated. If you expect equal pay and equal status on the job, you should also expect to be treated as an equal in other areas. For instance, a woman should be willing to open a door first if she arrives there before a man whether it is during or after work hours. However, if a man and woman arrive at the door at the same time, the man still opens the door. A woman should realize that a man often enjoys holding the door for her, and she can non-verbally indicate to him whether he should.

This mutual admiration society approach within the office can lessen the strain of doing something just because you are female.

In today's business world, the male/female relationships at work tend to be looked upon as those of colleagues, not as sex-oriented. This works well as long as both the man and woman feel comfortable in letting go of some previous manners taught, such as the woman expecting the man to help her with her coat or to always open the door for her. (Today a female employee can open the door for a senior executive unless he moves forward to open it for her.) Common sense should be used when it comes to such issues.

Handling Sexual Advances

This seems to be a problem not only with men approaching women, but with aggressive women approaching men. A good rule of thumb is to not give *any* suggestion of interest when an overture is obvious. It *does* take two to start any relationship.

Such things as a lingering eye contact or a handshake held too long can give cues without a word being said. If someone makes eye contact and lingers with a smile, simply look away and break that eye contact. If a man shakes hands and continues to "hold" hands, just take one step back. Your hand must follow and it will break the handshake.

If you are actually approached verbally, try reacting with humor rather than making an issue. Talking about your spouse or current date can discourage an attraction.

The important thing to remember is that relationships can begin very innocently with kind remarks and invitations to lunch or dinner.

Here are some professional ethics to keep in mind:

• Never accept advances of any kind from a married person.

• Dating clients is dangerous and un-professional unless the business relationship has come to an end and the social part of the relationship can be free from interfering with business.

- Dating the boss is awkward and inappropriate.

Male Customer's Compliments and Advances

As far as handling a male client's compliments, a simple "thank you" is all that is necessary. Handling advances can be done two ways — with humor or by ignoring them. Always remain gracious and professional and do not give any non-verbal clues of being interested.

In addition, try thinking of yourself as a professional who happens to be a woman rather than a woman who is trying to be professional. You will find that as you put this into practice, your response to these situations will be natural and effective without being offensive or unfeminine.

Refusing a Lunch Invitation

Refusing a luncheon with someone is your prerogative, whether in or outside of business. If you truly feel that a man has ulterior motives in asking you to lunch, you can simply state that you would prefer meeting at your office where your information is more readily available.

When you feel hesitant about going to lunch with a male client for this reason, it is probably better in the long run not to give any opportunity for misunderstood intentions. Keeping everything within business hours and the business setting is always appropriate.

The Role of the Female
Addressing the Female Peer

There are several names that should *not* be used by a man or another woman in referring to or addressing a woman: "girl," "dear," and "honey" are just a few.

Once when giving a presentation to a group of women, the speaker referred to them as "girls." Nothing was said at the time, but later she received a phone call from one of the women who had attended.

The attendee said, "If you don't mind my making a suggestion, don't ever call women 'girls.' It's demeaning. I have other friends in the business world who also dislike it. We're not girls — we're women." I have heard many comments from women executives that they just do not like being called "girls" under any circumstances.

If a man seems to be acting condescendingly toward you by calling you "honey," consider the man's attitude before you react. Some men have formed this habit long ago, see nothing wrong with it, and do not mean any disrespect by it. In this case, "honey" does not reflect how the man feels about you professionally. However, if you feel that the man is being condescending, do one of the following:

- Ignore what he said.
- Say, "My name is _____."
- Revert to calling him Mr. _____.
- Continue the business conversation and stick to facts.

Female/Female Relationships

The old idiom "It's lonely at the top" is true. Within any organization, there are defined levels. You cannot fully participate in two levels at the same time. You are either in management or on the support staff. You have to make a choice. You cannot maintain your identity at one level if you associate more comfortably and more obviously on another level. In other words, you cannot maintain a professional distance and be "one of the daily lunch group."

Many women in support roles have levels of informal power in the company. A secretary or receptionist can control whether you talk to her boss on the phone or get an appointment with him, she can relay your messages in a negative or positive manner, or she can fail to notify you of an important meeting. If you develop a good business relationship with her, she can pass on valuable tips to help you deal with her boss.

When dealing with a female who is in a lower position than you:

• Don't act condescendingly or demeaningly toward her.

• Don't patronize her or preach to her on how she should try for a more important position.

• Never confide any of your personal problems or matters to her and try to avoid learning any intimate details of her personal life. Keep all such conversations at a superficial level.

Wives of Male Associates

The wives may be concerned with potential intimate situations especially during out-of-town trips. Female business associates are sharing something with their husbands that wives cannot share in — his work. Keep this in mind whenever you are around the wives. Always be friendly and treat them with courtesy.

Entertaining a Male Client

A woman entertaining a male client can create an awkward situation unless she sets the mood and arranges the meeting appropriately. Some men may still be uncomfortable with women initiating the invitation. Here are a few suggestions to make things go smoothly for both parties:

1. When calling the man, make sure you tell him clearly that you would like to take him to lunch to discuss business. Say something like this, "Bob, I'd like to take you out to lunch and we can discuss this further." Or make the request in a neutral way by asking the client to let your company treat him to lunch. The woman executive is then seen as an agent of the company and not as a woman asking a man to lunch.

2. It is preferable to choose a restaurant you go to often, ideally a club where your company owns a membership, and arrange

ahead of time for the bill not be to brought to the table. Make the reservation in your name, and give the restaurant your credit card number ahead of time. Quickly excuse yourself during dessert and coffee to sign the check, or sign on the way out.

3. If you go to a restaurant where the bill must be brought to the table, simply quietly ask the waiter to have the check brought to you. Use a credit card to pay it. If the man insists on paying, it is best to let him, rather than make an issue of who should pay. If lunch meetings are frequent, you may want to alternate paying. (Incidentally, after signing a credit card receipt, pull off both carbons. This will eliminate any possibility of figure changes which might be made after you leave.)

4. Tipping should be added to include the usual 15 percent and perhaps an extra $1 or $2 if the headwaiter has been extra helpful.

5. If your colleague orders a cocktail, never feel you will offend him by ordering a Perrier or other non-alcoholic beverage. If you do not drink because of personal convictions, you should never feel second best because you choose not to drink.

Lunching with Other Women Employees

Decide ahead of time who will be in charge of the bill and pay the person your portion plus the tip when the bill arrives. Be very careful to do this quickly and generously. There is nothing more irritating to a waiter and to other women who are in a hurry to get back to work than to have to wait impatiently while someone tries to figure a portion of the bill to the penny.

Taking Another Woman to Lunch

If as a woman you call to ask another woman to have lunch with you, you should intend to pay the bill.

Be especially gracious in ordering as the guest of an entrepreneur. Remember, a business owner is *not* on a corporate account. Be respectful that prices may affect her company profit in a different way. (Incidentally, no matter what company your client is with, always order a moderately priced item unless he or she specifically suggests something expensive. Expense accounts are well monitored these days.)

The Corporate Wife

Leigh and her husband were planning to go to a reception of another company in order to get to know the people for business purposes. It was a very important occasion. My friend's husband was out of town and, due to bad weather, could not fly home in time to go to the reception.

Leigh certainly did not want to go without him, yet even without being able to talk to him about the situation, she knew that meeting the people at that reception was important to him. Leigh decided she would go alone. She chose an outfit that was conservative, but appropriate, and went.

At the reception, she introduced herself and explained that even though her husband had been detained, she had wanted to come alone to meet the people.

Making this special effort was one of the nicest things Leigh could have done for her husband. He asked her all kinds of questions about whom she had met and what the people were like. Also, the other company people were impressed to realize that the man's wife was so special. This woman knew what to do to support her husband in the way he needed it.

Behind a successful man is often a loving and supportive woman. Your role as your husband's support becomes more important the farther up the ladder of success he climbs. But how can you feel comfortable entertaining his clients and/or business colleagues? Here are some guidelines in the art of entertaining for you to follow and be a gracious hostess always:

• When planning to entertain and you feel a need for assistance from your husband's staff, ask your husband whom to contact and what responsibilities can be shared with you.

• Familiarize yourself with the business your husband is in and be able to speak the language when around his colleagues and clients. If he is in the high-tech industry, you should know the difference between hardware and software; in real estate, know something about the general market and interest rates; in advertising, understand market share, prime time, and layouts.

• Stay well read and knowledgeable about what is going on in your country, your city, and internationally.

• Stay informed of the latest fashions and continually upgrade your image to go along with his. Be sure you wear clothes that are currently in style and are appropriate to the occasion. Update your hairstyle and make-up periodically. Always reflect the best image you can for your husband's sake and yours.

• Celebrate his successes with a surprise candlelight dinner just for you two or an unannounced weekend getaway.

• Stay in good physical shape and get plenty of rest.

Mary, a very dear and special friend, is the epitome of a successful corporate wife. I asked her what she thought was the most important thing she does for her husband. She said, "I try to remember I'm not just a support to my husband, but rather I'm part of a team."

Mary has learned that his success becomes *their* success and together they share the reward.

CHAPTER 4

TRAVELING WITH COLLEAGUES OR ALONE

Traveling With a Senior Executive

As a junior executive, you should aide a senior executive as much as possible. Assist with details such as checking in and out of the hotel and tipping. Do not engage the senior executive in long conversations unless he encourages you.

When getting into a car or limousine, wait to take a seat until the senior executive has chosen one first.

When flying on a corporate jet, always arrive early. Board after the senior executive or host, and sit where you are shown. Do not ask for refreshments unless they are offered. Be neat when eating and drinking and do not litter.

Always thank the crew as you leave. Write a thank you note to the executive who reserved you a seat on the flight.

Male and Female Colleagues
Traveling Together

When men and women travel together on business, certain behavior should be followed for the sake of reputation. Here are some basic guidelines.

1. Avoid flirtations, no matter how innocent. They may be misunderstood.

2. At the first sign of inappropriate behavior on the part of your colleague, take some action to end it right there. Then act as though the incident never happened to preserve the working relationship.

3. When business needs to be conducted, arrange to work in a public place such as the hotel lobby or restaurant.

4. A man and a woman should be separately responsible for expenses.

• A woman executive should travel with advance money or use her own money to pay for her expenses, then later be reimbursed by her company.

• If a male and female colleague dine together, they should each use their own expense account to pay for their meal.

• A woman executive should tip for her own baggage handling and airport limousine fee.

• Either the man or woman may pay shared taxi fares, then reimbursements should be made for filing individual expense reports.

A Woman Traveling Alone on Business

Business travel is a special concern for women. Your travel objectives, however, are the same as for the male executive. You have a job to do and you want to do that job efficiently, minimizing time, energy, cost, and aggravation while maximizing your comfort and enjoyment.

Safety/Danger Zones and Times

When traveling alone, establish safety/danger zones and times. For instance:

Safety zones — your hotel room, the front desk, the coffee shop.

Danger zones — the bar, elevators, stairways, parking lot, garages, and hallways. While in these areas, stay alert to signs of danger.

Safety times — daylight. Make your flight reservations early in the day and arrive at your destination before dark.

Dining

Many women who travel tell me that they do not feel comfortable dining alone in a restaurant and, for that reason, often use room service. By eating in their room, they accomplish more work, but often would rather be among people.

As a businesswoman, you have every right to dine alone in a restaurant. Walk in confidently and say, "Dinner for one, please." They key is to act as if you belong there and deserve the same good service given to everyone else.

If the service is good, leave a tip of 15 to 20 percent. Also keep in mind when figuring the tip that there is no such thing as a table for one. If your waiter had served two people, the check would have been twice as big.

If you intend to be left alone while dining, try the following:

1. Remain businesslike in your dress and behavior. You could even carry your briefcase or other papers. Both actions clearly give the message that you are a professional businesswoman and are involved in reviewing business while you are eating.

2. Handle intrusions diplomatically.

If someone you are not interested in talking to starts talking to you, smile pleasantly and answer him, then take papers from your briefcase and begin working.

If someone asks to join you and you want to refuse, simply say, "No thanks."

If you prefer not to travel alone, look into traveling with someone else in your organization or with a group. You might be able to travel with other females from other companies who are going to the same place at the same time.

Hotels
Precautions

When staying in a hotel or motel, both men and women should take certain precautions, but women should be especially careful.

1. Avoid exposing your room number in a public setting such as in a restaurant when signing your check.

2. Always double lock your room door and put on the chain. Check balcony doors and windows. If one is broken or cannot be locked, call for a maintenance man to fix it or show you how to lock it.

3. Do not enter your room if people are standing idly nearby. Walk past your door, then return later. When leaving your room, look carefully down the hallway as a precaution. Always check to be sure the door has locked behind you.

Tipping

When checking out of a hotel, tip the bellman $1 per bag or $1 for the first bag and $.50 for smaller bags. Rather than tipping per bag, you may give a general tip of $3 to $5.

Tip the valet attendant who brings your car $2 minimum — $1 for bringing the car and $1 per bag.

CHAPTER 5

PLANNING CORPORATE ENTERTAINMENT

The days of the unlimited expense account are no longer the norm. Corporations are cutting back in every financial area. For this reason, they are watching more closely the business person's expense account. Highly visible business entertainment, weekend getaways, and inclusion of family and friends are no longer common.

When done correctly, entertaining is one of the most productive tools available to the business person. Billions of dollars are spent each year for entertaining to create additional business for the company. Business entertaining is not just fun — it is profitable. Cost effectiveness of entertaining *is* a consideration.

Reasons for Entertaining

1. To form relationships which will lead toward further business between two companies.

2. To express gratitude. Treating someone to an expensive formal dinner or even a simple lunch is a good way of saying, "Thank you."

3. To celebrate a business success. Reward yourself and others for a job well done.

4. To help make decisions. Sometimes getting away from the office atmosphere allows people to think more openly and objectively when a difficult decision needs to be made.

The Key Ingredient

Careful planning is the key ingredient to successful entertaining. There are so many details that it is important to write everything down.

Make sure you have remembered to arrange every detail as well as to remember what details you have arranged! Your written plans can be a valuable resource when you analyze the success of your business entertaining and plan future events, whether large or small. In planning a party consider: business objectives, cost, and time commitment.

Tips for the Good Host

Being considerate of your guests is the most important prerequisite for any host or hostess.

Mary, who entertains frequently with her executive husband, has learned to plan events and allow enough time for people's relaxation as well. Packing an agenda full of entertaining is not relaxing or fun without including personal time for them to do what they choose.

There are certain how-to's that apply to every situation in which you will entertain:

• Select a location for the event which will be comfortable for the guests. The area should be cool and well ventilated. Music should be pleasant and soft.

• Plan the arrangement of the buffet table and beverage service areas, and the seating and reception line to facilitate the movement of guests.

• See that adequate serving utensils, napkins, and other service items are available.

• Consult with your caterer to determine the types and amount of beverages to serve for the length of the party and the tastes of your guests.

- Select tablecloths, napkins, floral arrangements, and serving pieces that are interesting. Arrange dishes, utensils, and serving pieces artfully on the table.

- Use as many flowers as your budget will allow. A good florist will help you enhance the table decor.

The Always Rules

- Treat every guest as a VIP (very important person).

- Always ask if your guests would like to participate in a certain activity you have planned.

- Plan events that you know your guests will enjoy. For example, some guests may prefer a Western barbecue to a formal sit-down dinner.

- Be sure there is sufficient room and plenty of chairs.

- Offer a variety of beverages.

- If you notice that a guest is not touching some of his food, ask him if he would like more of the items that he has eaten. Never put your guest on the spot by asking him why he has not eaten something.

• Food, beverages, service, and entertainment should be top quality.

• To cut down on expenses, invite fewer guests, select less-expensive foods, or serve fewer courses — never sacrifice quality.

Be a gracious host! Smile. Mingle with your guests. Visit with everyone. Introduce newcomers and see that shy guests are put at ease.

• In your home, provide the restrooms with guest towels, fancy soaps, and other special items.

• Never make an issue of something that went wrong in front of your guests.

• Make sure that your dishes, utensils, and serving pieces sparkle.

• All service personnel should be impeccably groomed. Uniforms should be spotless and pressed. Hair and nails must be well manicured.

Menu Planning

Because food is the most important component of a successful formal meal, the menu should be planned with great care.

The number of courses you serve is dependent upon the importance of the occasion and the size of your budget. Naturally, for very important affairs, prepare the most elaborate meal you can afford. A formal luncheon should consist of two to three courses and a formal dinner, of three to seven courses.

Two to Seven Course Meals

Two Course Meal

1. Salad, vegetable, meat
2. Dessert

Three Course

1. Appetizer or soup
2. Salad, vegetable, meat
3. Dessert

Four Course

1. Appetizer or soup.
2. Salad
3. Vegetable, meat
4. Dessert

Five Course

1. Appetizer
2. Soup
3. Salad
4. Vegetable, meat
5. Dessert

Six Course

1. Appetizer
2. Soup
3. Fish
4. Vegetable, meat
5. Green salad and cheese
6. Dessert

Seven Course

1. Appetizer
2. Soup
3. Fish
4. Sorbet
5. Vegetable, meat
6. Green salad and cheese
7. Dessert

• Make sure your menu is suitable for your guests' appetites and tastes, the type of event, and the time of day and year. Serve hearty, hot dishes in the winter and light, cool ones in the summer. Never serve finger food and dainties to a group of men or *steak tartare* to a group of women.

• Select foods within your budget. Berries out of season should not be added. If you need to watch your budget, select easily attainable foods.

• The food must awaken the taste buds and please the eye.

- Select as many fresh foods as possible.

- Plan nutritious meals. Avoid fried or heavily sauced foods.

- Select foods with a variety of tastes, colors, textures, and temperatures.

    *Since many people are controlling serious health problems with special diets, the wise host should ask his guests if they have any special dietary restrictions. This can be conveniently done when extending invitations or receiving RSVP's by telephone.

"Part II" is from *Corporate Protocol — A Brief Case for Business Etiquette* by Valetie Grant-Sokolosky (Tulsa: Harrison House, 1986), pp. 97-102, 167-176, 195-199.

PART III

FOR THE WORKING MOTHER

By
Edwin Louis Cole
and
Nancy Corbett Cole

"True womanhood can never be measured
by a man's affections or society's praises,
but by a woman's own character as
measured by the Word of God."

Nancy Corbett Cole

CHAPTER 6

TWO CAREERS:
BUSINESS AND MOTHER

While contemplating ministry in the home and motherhood, I happened to be on the telephone talking to my daughter, Lois. She and her husband, Rick, have given us two of the most beautiful, brilliant, lovable and enjoyable granddaughters the world has ever seen. And if you think I am prejudiced, you are right!

While I was talking to her, I asked her what being a mother meant to her. This was her reply: "Being a mother means never having a free moment even on vacations. It means being responsible for little people twenty-four hours a day with never a day off!"

I chimed in with the observation that even when our children are in their thirties, as Lois is, the responsibility is still there. We both laughed. She and I enjoy motherhood. I do not know of anyone who enjoys her children more or is a better mother without stress or strain than Lois. However, the fact of the matter is that we touched on a sober reality: motherhood is a full-time job that never ends! Being a mother is a great and awesome responsibility. Many of us get married and can hardly wait for that first baby. All we can think of is that soft warm, tiny mass of humanity.

What women usually do not think about are the sleepless nights, the mounds of dirty diapers, the feeding difficulties, the colic, and all those other unpleasant things that rear their ugly heads during the course of infancy and the toddler stage.

"Will this ever end?" may be a mother's cry! The answer is obvious. Barring calamity, no it will never end. But the joys of motherhood far outweigh the burden of responsibility.

Mothers imprint their attitudes and ideas onto the child's young, immature life. So it is very important what we are putting into that child. Are you implanting a fearful, critical attitude or a peaceful, loving, forgiving, God-fearing nature?

When my children were young, I guess I made every mistake a new mother can make. I am sure I was short-tempered at times. None of us is perfect. But, *it is what we do with our failures that counts*. Do we take them to the Lord and ask for forgiveness? Do we ask our children to forgive us when necessary?

Our attitudes toward the children and the constancy of living a godly life day by day are what will stay in their minds and hearts. That is what will give them a security in their identity to carry them through the crises and good times of later years. Providing you have worked on putting a God-consciousness into their spirits, they will have the marvelous assurance of who they are in God.

Also remember that each of your children has a different, unique personality. When Paul, as a young teenager, spent hours playing the guitar in his room, I had no idea he was composing songs that later blessed our congregation and others with their purity and simplicity.

Nor did I recognize Lois' propensity for debate (which sometimes we called "arguing") that presaged a successful career as a prosecuting attorney.

With Joann, I remember seeing her tie her shoes at a very early age, before kindergarten, and I was ashamed that I had not even tried to teach her that skill which she learned by herself. Then in fifth grade, there was talk of skipping her to seventh grade. I realized she was smart, but what I did not realize was her extraordinary sensitivity to the world around her. Not until she was through school and going through a turbulent time spiritually did I develop an awareness that she, and the other children were made up of spirit, soul and body, each uniquely different from the others.

My children still surprise me with some of the qualities they exhibit. I think, "Where did they ever learn that?" We have to remember we may not always see our children as they really are in God's eyes. We must discipline ourselves in prayer to learn what "makes them tick."

Edwin and I do not have a perfect family, but we have stayed on our knees and God has been faithful. If you think you, or your children, cannot live up to God's greatest goals for your lives, quit trying to do it on your own. Let God be strong within you, instead of trying to be strong for Him. We cannot impress God. But we are impressed by Him when we see what He makes of our lives. Release your children to God and allow them to achieve.

My daughters have struggled with being working mothers as I did. I have noticed, however, that every woman in Scripture worked or held some kind of title, although not always for pay. Every mother must examine her own heart about working outside the home, whether as a volunteer or for pay. What a fallacy to call a full-time homemaker a nonworking mother!

There are women who prefer outside involvement, even though they do not have to work. The Bible certainly teaches it is better to be busy than idle and that godly women adorn themselves with good works. Idleness leads to gossip. It also leads to fantasy and sexual immorality. So the choice of occupying yourself with work or not is up to you, although the priorities of family first never change.

If you find yourself in the workplace earning a living for any reason, then by all means, get the best job possible, preferably one with a chance for advancement. If you have the talent and brains for a high-level job and the opportunity is there, then go for it! If you have to be away from your family anyway, at least make those hours worth your time, and theirs.

There is a pitfall in career planning, however, which you will have to keep in balance — and that is the cost to your family.

Lois was in line for a promotion but in observing the people already in that coveted post, she saw this would be a very time-consuming position that would require long hours both in the office and at home. She had had a taste of this occasionally and it troubled her. Once when she was engaged in some extra, very intensive work, she told me that even though she would go home to be with her family, she was so preoccupied, she would not hear them when they attempted to converse with her. In one instance her troubled little girl said, "Mom! I have asked you the same question five times, and you didn't hear me even once."

When the time came for the promotion, Lois very prayerfully and conscientiously turned it down. Since then, she and Rick have moved to an entirely new community where their workplaces are closer to home and their daughters' schools, and Lois is in an even more exciting position! God does lead and guide us, as He has promised in His Word.

Whether you are working or not, every mother wonders at times if she is losing patience or sanity. A few years ago, I was visiting my son when his youngest child was barely three years old. My daughter-in-law, Judi, was being a lovely hostess and making sure I was comfortable.

The first morning she scurried around the kitchen serving waffles to us all. When she handed me my plate, I looked down at a sight that would make a pre-schooler drool: buttered waffles covered with syrup and cut into bite-sized pieces. When Judi saw me hesitate, she looked at the plate and realized what she had done. We all laughed uproariously. Cutting everyone's food is the classic blooper of a mother of small children!

Judi found that being home continually with her children caused her mind to stagnate and her social skills to diminish. So she worked sporadically, choosing her own hours as a makeup artist, and finally started a business out of her own house. Now she is able to be with the children but have outside interests as well.

A mother with young children must be careful lest the cares of the world choke the life, or spirit out of her. When the pressure is on, it is easy to develop bad habits. One of those is to take out frustrations on the children. We must learn to accept our weaknesses as ours and not blame the children because we have let anxiety or pressure mount.

On the other hand, we cannot wait and let the father deal with the more serious issues. "Just wait until your father gets home!" is a phrase that, with a little bit of contemplation and calmness, could so often be avoided. A working father comes home from a turbulent world wanting a peaceful haven. He does not need his children dreading his return home, nor does he need a blow-by-blow account of every detail of the day.

The relationship with your children must never become a stumbling block to the relationship with your husband. Children need the benefits of a good marriage between their father and mother.

A common complaint among young mothers is the massive amount of work —

cleaning up after more and more people in the house, mounds of laundry, hungry mouths to feed three times a day. Most young mothers lead strenuous lives. But if you plan carefully, and train the children (and your husband!) to help, you can do it. I was surprised to read a doctor's report suggesting that by eight years of age children should be responsible for cleaning their own bedrooms, and by ten they should be able to do any major chore around the house, even vacuuming.

I discovered this for myself when my children were very small. Many a night as we pioneered a new church with three children under four years of age, I crawled into bed on legs that felt hollowed out and barely functionable. I will never forget the feeling! Then Edwin began ministering as a missionary-evangelist and was frequently away on trips that lasted days, weeks, and sometimes months. To add to the difficulty of being alone with the children, I worked full time and drove an hour each way to work. Those were not easy years, but God gave me wisdom.

I realized that if I wanted the children to help me with chores when they were older, I might as well start right then. (Later I discovered this was scriptural! — Hebrews 12:11.) So on Saturday mornings, they each had an assignment. Even the youngest at five years old had a dust cloth and dusted the entire house herself. Granted, I had to go behind them and pick up what they missed after they were in bed at night, but after a few years of investing this way, I reaped big dividends. They all became valuable helps to me around the house.

There is only one regret that remains from those years, and that is when Paul showed an interest in cooking, I did not teach him. (Yes, I confess to stereotyped thinking!) Not only did I live to regret stifling that creative outlet, but so does his wife, Judi!

Another thing God showed me during that time was how to spend time alone with Him regardless of how full my days were. The plan He gave me was both simple and effective once I implemented it. Here it is: I put the children to bed earlier!

I knew Paul had a flashlight under his covers and he was reading, and I could hear Lois and Joann giggling. Nevertheless, I was marvelously alone for a few quiet moments in the evenings to enjoy the Lord — just Him and me. That relationship is the most important to keep intact.

As Edwin says, "It is more important to talk to the Lord about your children than to your children about the Lord."

One more thing I want to add: Did you ever treat your child or children in a way you had vowed never to treat them? Perhaps your parents treated you that way, and long ago you vowed you would never do the same thing. If this has happened to you, examine your heart for unforgiveness toward your parents. You may hardly be aware of the resentment that you still feel over those incidents that disturbed you. When you become aware of hidden resentments, you can be released by forgiving those who hurt you, whether they are still living or not, and asking the Lord to take it out of your life.

Overall, it is your attitude toward your child that will linger on. An attitude of appreciation toward children is what I suggest as the antidote for attitudes of resentment, jealousy, or frustration. Choose to appreciate the great attributes God has placed within the life of each one.

Thank God every day for your husband and/or children. They are His gifts to you. Thank Him for your home. Thank Him for the peace that He floods your heart with. Psalm 91, Isaiah 65:24, John 15:7, First Chronicles 16:11, Psalms 25:5, and Isaiah 30:15 are great scriptures to start the day with as you prepare to minister in the home.

"Part III" is from *The Unique Woman* by Edwin Louis Cole and Nancy Corbett Cole (Tulsa: Honor Books, 1989), pp. 150-156.

A GUIDE TO "GOLDEN RULE MANAGEMENT"

By
Mary Kay Ash

"Success consists of a series
of little daily efforts."

Mamie McCullough

CHAPTER 7

MARY KAY'S SECRET OF SUCCESS

This is the management philosophy that turned Mary Kay Ash's storefront cosmetics business into a multimillion dollar corporation in just twenty years. Based on the age-old Golden Rule, it encourages managers to treat staff, customers, suppliers — everyone — with the same care, consideration and concern they would like to receive themselves. It brought spectacular success to Mary Kay. Here's how it can work for you.

• **Recognize the Value of People.** People are your company's number one asset. When you treat them as you would like to be treated yourself, everyone benefits.

• **Praise Your People to Success.** Recognition is the most powerful of all motivators. Even criticism can build confidence when it's "sandwiched" between layers of praise.

- **Tear Down That Ivory Tower.** Keep all doors open. Be accessible to everyone. Remember that every good manager is also a good listener.

- **Be a Risk-Taker.** Don't be afraid. Encourage your people to take risks, too — and allow room for error.

- **Be Sales Oriented.** Nothing happens in business until somebody sells something. Be especially sensitive to your customers' needs and desires.

- **Be a Problem-Solver.** An effective manager knows how to recognize real problems and how to take action to solve them.

- **Create a Stress-Free Workplace.** By eliminating stress factors — fear of the boss, unreasonable deadlines, and others — you can increase and inspire productivity.

- **Develop and Promote People from Within.** Upward mobility for employees in your company builds loyalty. People give you their best when they know they'll be rewarded.

- **Keep Business in Its Proper Place.** At May Kay Cosmetics the order of priorities is faith, family, and career. The real key to success is creating an environment where people are encouraged to balance the many aspects of their lives.

"Part IV" is from *May Kay on People Management* by Mary Kay Ash, copyright © 1984 by Mary Kay Cosmetics, Inc. (New York: Warner Books, Inc.), back cover.

PART V

WISDOM AND INSPIRATION THROUGH THE SCRIPTURES

Your word is a lamp to my feet
and a light for my path.

Psalm 119:105

CHAPTER 8

THE BUSINESSWOMAN AND HER ATTITUDE

The Faith of a Businesswoman

Those who know your name will trust in you, for you, LORD, have never forsaken those who seek you.

Psalm 9:10

Trust in the LORD and do good; dwell in the land and enjoy safe pasture.

Delight yourself in the LORD and he will give you the desires of your heart.

Commit your way to the LORD; trust in him and he will do this.

Psalm 37:3-5

You will keep in perfect peace him whose mind is steadfast, because he trusts in you.

Isaiah 26:3

But blessed is the man who trusts in the LORD, whose confidence is in him.

Jeremiah 17:7

When he had gone indoors, the blind men came to him, and he asked them, "Do you believe that I am able to do this?" "Yes, Lord," they replied.

Then he touched their eyes and said, "According to your faith will it be done to you."

Matthew 9:28,29

He replied, "Because you have so little faith. I tell you the truth, if you have faith as small as a mustard seed, you can say to this mountain, 'Move from here to there' and it will move. Nothing will be impossible for you."

Matthew 17:20

If you believe, you will receive whatever you ask for in prayer.

Matthew 21:22

"'If you can'?" said Jesus. "Everything is possible for him who believes."

Mark 9:23

"Have faith in God," Jesus answered.

"I tell you the truth, if anyone says to this mountain, 'Go, throw yourself into the sea,' and does not doubt in his heart but believes that what he says will happen, it will be done for him.

Therefore I tell you, whatever you ask for in prayer, believe that you have received it, and it will be yours."

Mark 11:22-24

Consequently, faith comes from hearing the message, and the message is heard through the word of Christ.

Romans 10:17

For by the grace given me I say to every one of you: Do not think of yourself more highly than you ought, but rather think of yourself with sober judgment, in accordance with the measure of faith God has given you.

Romans 12:3

In addition to all this, take up the shield of faith, with which you can extinguish all the flaming arrows of the evil one.

Ephesians 6:16

So do not throw away your confidence; it will be richly rewarded.

Hebrews 10:35

Now faith is being sure of what we hope for and certain of what we do not see.

And without faith it is impossible to please God, because anyone who comes to him must believe that he exists and that he rewards those who earnestly seek him.

Hebrews 11:1,6

Let us fix our eyes on Jesus, the author and perfecter of our faith, who for the joy set before him endured the cross, scorning its shame, and sat down at the right hand of the throne of God.

Hebrews 12:2

Keep your lives free from the love of money and be content with what you have, because God has said, "Never will I leave you; never will I forsake you."

So we say with confidence, "The LORD is my helper; I will not be afraid. What can man do to me?"

Hebrews 13:5,6

And the prayer offered in faith will make the sick person well; the LORD will raise him up. If he has sinned, he will be forgiven.

James 5:15

These have come so that your faith — of greater worth than gold, which perishes even though refined by fire — may be proved genuine and may result in praise, glory and honor when Jesus Christ is revealed.

Though you have not seen him, you love him; and even though you do not see him now, you believe in him and are filled with an inexpressible and glorious joy,

For you are receiving the goal of your faith, the salvation of your souls.

1 Peter 1:7-9

For everyone born of God overcomes the world. This is the victory that has overcome the world, even our faith.

1 John 5:4

The Motivation of a Businesswoman

Be strong and courageous. Do not be afraid or terrified because of them, for the LORD your God goes with you; he will never leave you nor forsake you.

Deuteronomy 31:6

Be strong and courageous, because you will lead these people to inherit the land I swore to their forefathers to give them.

Joshua 1:6

The LORD has driven out before you great and powerful nations; to this day no one has been able to withstand you.

Joshua 23:9

David was greatly distressed because the men were talking of stoning him; each one was bitter in spirit because of his sons and daughters. But David found strength in the LORD his God.

1 Samuel 30:6

"Don't be afraid," the prophet answered. "Those who are with us are more than those who are with them."

2 Kings 6:16

Through you we push back our enemies; through your name we trample our foes.

Psalm 44:5

Instruct a wise man and he will be wiser still; teach a righteous man and he will add to his learning.

Proverbs 9:9

If a man is lazy, the rafters sag; if his hands are idle, the house leaks.

Ecclesiastes 10:18

For I am the LORD, your God, who takes hold of your right hand and says to you, Do not fear; I will help you.

Isaiah 41:13

Those who are wise will shine like the brightness of the heavens, and those who lead many to righteousness, like the stars for ever and ever.

Daniel 12:3

Ask and it will be given to you; seek and you will find; knock and the door will be opened to you.

For everyone who asks receives; he who seeks finds; and to him who knocks, the door will be opened.

Matthew 7:7,8

And I tell you that you are Peter, and on this rock I will build my church, and the gates of Hades will not overcome it.

I will give you the keys of the kingdom of heaven; whatever you bind on earth will be bound in heaven, and whatever you loose on earth will be loosed in heaven.

Matthew 16:18,19

I tell you the truth, anyone who has faith in me will do what I have been doing. He will do even greater things than these, because I am going to the Father.

John 14:12

But you will receive power when the Holy Spirit comes on you; and you will be my witnesses in Jerusalem, and in all Judea and Samaria, and to the ends of the earth.

Acts 1:8

The weapons we fight with are not the weapons of the world. On the contrary, they have divine power to demolish strongholds.

2 Corinthians 10:4

For it is light that makes everything visible. This is why it is said: "Wake up, O sleeper, rise from the dead, and Christ will shine on you."

Ephesians 5:14

I can do everything through him who gives me strength.

Philippians 4:13

What, then, shall we say in response to this? If God is for us, who can be against us?

Romans 8:31

Being strengthened with all power according to his glorious might so that you may have great endurance and patience, and joyfully giving thanks to the Father, who has qualified you to share in the inheritance of the saints in the kingdom of light.

Colossians 1:11,12

Be wise in the way you act toward outsiders; make the most of every opportunity.

Colossians 4:5

Be diligent in these matters; give yourself wholly to them, so that everyone may see your progress.

1 Timothy 4:15

Therefore let us leave the elementary teachings about Christ and go on to maturity.

Hebrews 6:1a

You, dear children, are from God and have overcome them, because the one who is in you is greater than the one who is in the world.

We are from God, and whoever knows God listens to us; but whoever is not from God does not listen to us. This is how we recognize the Spirit of truth and the spirit of falsehood.

And so we know and rely on the love God has for us. God is love. Whoever lives in love lives in God, and God in him.

In this way, love is made complete among us so that we will have confidence on the day of judgment, because in this world we are like him.

1 John 4:4,6,16,17

Dear friend, I pray that you may enjoy good health and that all may go well with you, even as your soul is getting along well.

3 John 2

The Integrity of a Businesswoman

As for you, if you walk before me in integrity of heart and uprightness, as David your father did, and do all I command and observe my decrees and laws, I will establish your royal throne over Israel forever, as I promised David your father when I said, "You shall never fail to have a man on the throne of Israel."

1 Kings 9:4,5

Let God weigh me in honest scales and he will know that I am blameless.

Job 31:6

Blessed is the man who does not walk in the counsel of the wicked or stand in the way of sinners or sit in the seat of mockers.

But his delight is in the law of the LORD, and on his law he meditates day and night.

Psalm 1:1,2

All the ways of the LORD are loving and faithful for those who keep the demands of his covenant.

May integrity and uprightness protect me, because my hope is in you.

Psalm 25:10,21

Vindicate me, O LORD, for I have led a blameless life; I have trusted in the LORD without wavering.

Psalm 26:1

In my integrity you uphold me and set me in your presence forever.

Psalm 41:12

And David shepherded them with integrity of heart; with skillful hands he led them.

Psalm 78:72

Good will come to him who is generous and lends freely, who conducts his affairs with justice.

Psalm 112:5

Blessed are they who keep his statutes and seek him with all their heart.

You have laid down precepts that are to be fully obeyed.

Psalm 119:2,4

The LORD abhors dishonest scales, but accurate weights are his delight.

The integrity of the upright guides them, but the unfaithful are destroyed by their duplicity.

Proverbs 11:1,3

Better a little with righteousness than much gain with injustice.

Proverbs 16:8

Better a poor man whose walk is blameless than a fool whose lips are perverse.

He who obeys instructions guards his life, but he who is contemptuous of his ways will die.

Proverbs 19:1,16

The righteous man leads a blameless life; blessed are his children after him.

Proverbs 20:7

A fortune made by a lying tongue is a fleeting vapor and a deadly snare.

Proverbs 21:6

If you are willing and obedient, you will eat the best from the land.

Isaiah 1:19

Do not repay anyone evil for evil. Be careful to do what is right in the eyes of everybody.

Romans 12:17

Wise Counsel and the Businesswoman

Blessed is the man who does not walk in the counsel of the wicked or stand in the way of sinners or sit in the seat of mockers.

But his delight is in the law of the LORD, and on his law he meditates day and night.

He is like a tree planted by streams of water, which yields its fruit in season and whose leaf does not wither. Whatever he does prospers.

Psalm 1:1-3

I will praise the LORD, who counsels me; even at night my heart instructs me.

Psalm 16:7

Show me your ways, O LORD, teach me your paths.

Psalm 25:4

Though an army besiege me, my heart will not fear; though war break out against me, even then will I be confident.

One thing I ask of the LORD, this is what I seek: that I may dwell in the house of the LORD all the days of my life, to gaze upon the beauty of the LORD and to seek him in his temple.

For in the day of trouble he will keep me safe in his dwelling; he will hide me in the shelter of his tabernacle and set me high upon a rock.

Psalm 27:3-5

I will instruct you and teach you in the way you should go; I will counsel you and watch over you.

Psalm 32:8

God is our refuge and strength, an ever-present help in trouble.

Psalm 46:1

Surely you desire truth in the inner parts; you teach me wisdom in the inmost place.

Psalm 51:6

I will say of the LORD, "He is my refuge and my fortress, my God, in whom I trust."

Psalm 91:2

Even in darkness light dawns for the upright, for the gracious and compassionate and righteous man.

Psalm 112:4

The LORD is with me; I will not be afraid. What can man do to me?

It is better to take refuge in the LORD than to trust in man.

Psalm 118:6,8

Your word, O LORD, is eternal; it stands firm in the heavens.

Psalm 119:89

For the LORD gives wisdom, and from his mouth come knowledge and understanding.

Proverbs 2:6

Trust in the LORD with all your heart and lean not on your own understanding;

In all your ways acknowledge him, and he will make your paths straight.

Proverbs 3:5,6

My son, pay attention to what I say; listen closely to my words.

Do not let them out of your sight, keep them within your heart;

For they are life to those who find them and health to a man's whole body.

Proverbs 4:20-22

For lack of guidance a nation falls, but many advisers make victory sure.

Proverbs 11:14

Plans fail for lack of counsel, but with many advisers they succeed.

Proverbs 15:22

Perfume and incense bring joy to the heart, and the pleasantness of one's friend springs from his earnest counsel.

Proverbs 27:9

Whether you turn to the right or to the left, your ears will hear a voice behind you, saying, "This is the way; walk in it."

Isaiah 30:21

The grass withers and the flowers fall, but the word of our God stands forever.

Isaiah 40:8

I will lead the blind by ways they have not known, along unfamiliar paths I will guide them; I will turn the darkness into light before them and make the rough places smooth. These are the things I will do; I will not forsake them.

Isaiah 42:16

This is what the LORD says — your Redeemer, the Holy One of Israel: "I am the LORD your God, who teaches you what is best for you, who directs you in the way you should go."

Isaiah 48:17

I tell you the truth, this generation will certainly not pass away until all these things have happened.

Matthew 24:34

But when he, the Spirit of truth, comes, he will guide you into all truth. He will not speak on his own; he will speak only what he hears, and he will tell you what is yet to come.

He will bring glory to me by taking from what is mine and making it known to you.

John 16:13,14

What, then, shall we say in response to this? If God is for us, who can be against us?

Romans 8:31

If any of you lacks wisdom, he should ask God, who gives generously to all without finding fault, and it will be given to him.

James 1:5

CHAPTER 9

THE BUSINESSWOMAN AND HER CAREER

Helping an Employee Who Is Hurting

The Sovereign LORD has given me an instructed tongue, to know the word that sustains the weary. He wakens me morning by morning, wakens my ear to listen like one being taught.

Isaiah 50:4

Is not this the kind of fasting I have chosen: to loose the chains of injustice and untie the cords of the yoke, to set the oppressed free and break every yoke?

Is it not to share your food with the hungry and to provide the poor wanderer with shelter — when you see the naked, to clothe him, and not to turn away from your own flesh and blood?

Isaiah 58:6,7

So in everything, do to others what you would have them do to you, for this sums up the Law and the Prophets.

Matthew 7:12

And the second is like it: "Love your neighbor as yourself."

Matthew 22:39

Then the King will say to those on his right, "Come, you who are blessed by my Father; take your inheritance, the kingdom prepared for you since the creation of the world.

For I was hungry and you gave me something to eat, I was thirsty and you gave me something to drink, I was a stranger and you invited me in,

I needed clothes and you clothed me, I was sick and you looked after me, I was in prison and you came to visit me."

Matthew 25:34-36

By this all men will know that you are my disciples, if you love one another.

John 13:35

In everything I did, I showed you that by this kind of hard work we must help the weak, remembering the words the LORD Jesus himself said: "It is more blessed to give than to receive."

Acts 20:35

Rejoice with those who rejoice; mourn with those who mourn.

Romans 12:15

We who are strong ought to bear with the failings of the weak and not to please ourselves.

Romans 15:1

Praise be to the God and Father of our LORD Jesus Christ, the Father of compassion and the God of all comfort,

Who comforts us in all our troubles, so that we can comfort those in any trouble with the comfort we ourselves have received from God.

For just as the sufferings of Christ flow over into our lives, so also through Christ our comfort overflows.

2 Corinthians 1:3-5

Carry each other's burdens, and in this way you will fulfill the law of Christ.

Galatians 6:2

Remember those in prison as if you were their fellow prisoners, and those who are mistreated as if you yourselves were suffering.

And do not forget to do good and to share with others, for with such sacrifices God is pleased.

Hebrews 13:3,16

If you really keep the royal law found in Scripture, "Love your neighbor as yourself," you are doing right.

James 2:8

Finally, all of you, live in harmony with one another; be sympathetic, love as brothers, be compassionate and humble.

1 Peter 3:8

When Faced With Terminating an Employee

The LORD turn his face toward you and give you peace.

Numbers 6:26

For the LORD your God is a merciful God; he will not abandon or destroy you or forget the covenant with your forefathers, which he confirmed to them by oath.

Deuteronomy 4:31

Be strong and courageous. Do not be afraid or terrified because of them, for the LORD your God goes with you; he will never leave you nor forsake you.

The LORD himself goes before you and will be with you; he will never leave you nor forsake you. Do not be afraid; do not be discouraged.

Deuteronomy 31:6,8

I am still confident of this: I will see the goodness of the LORD in the land of the living.

Wait for the LORD; be strong and take heart and wait for the LORD.

Psalm 27:13,14

Let your face shine on your servant; save me in your unfailing love.

Psalm 31:16

I was young and now I am old, yet I have never seen the righteous forsaken or their children begging bread.

Psalm 37:25

Therefore I tell you, do not worry about your life, what you will eat or drink; or about your body, what you will wear. Is not life more important than food, and the body more important than clothes?

Therefore do not worry about tomorrow, for tomorrow will worry about itself. Each day has enough trouble of its own.

Matthew 6:25,34

May the God of hope fill you with all joy and peace as you trust in him, so that you may overflow with hope by the power of the Holy Spirit.

Romans 15:13

No temptation has seized you except what is common to man. And God is faithful; he will not let you be tempted beyond what you can bear. But when you are tempted, he will also provide a way out so that you can stand up under it.

1 Corinthians 10:13

Finally, be strong in the LORD and in his mighty power.

Ephesians 6:10

I am not saying this because I am in need, for I have learned to be content whatever the circumstances.

I know what it is to be in need, and I know what it is to have plenty. I have learned the secret of being content in any and every situation, whether well fed or hungry, whether living in plenty or in want.

I can do everything through him who gives me strength.

And my God will meet all your needs according to his glorious riches in Christ Jesus.

Philippians 4:11-13,19

Never will I leave you; never will I forsake you.

Hebrews 13:5b

These have come so that your faith — of greater worth than gold, which perishes even though refined by fire — may be proved genuine and may result in praise, glory and honor when Jesus Christ is revealed.

1 Peter 1:7

Dealing With Betrayal at Work

Teach me your way, O LORD; lead me in a straight path because of my oppressors.

Wait for the LORD; be strong and take heart and wait for the LORD.

Psalm 27:11,14

For I hear the slander of many; there is terror on every side; they conspire against me and plot to take my life.

My times are in your hands; deliver me from my enemies and from those who pursue me.

Let your face shine on your servant; save me in your unfailing love.

Psalm 31:13,15,16

The angel of the LORD encamps around those who fear him, and he delivers them.

Taste and see that the LORD is good; blessed is the man who takes refuge in him.

Psalm 34:7,8

Ruthless witnesses come forward; they question me on things I know nothing about.

They repay me evil for good and leave my soul forlorn.

Yet when they were ill, I put on sackcloth and humbled myself with fasting. When my prayers returned to me unanswered,

I went about mourning as though for my friend or brother. I bowed my head in grief as though weeping for my mother.

But when I stumbled, they gathered in glee; attackers gathered against me when I was unaware. They slandered me without ceasing.

Let not those gloat over me who are my enemies without cause; let not those who hate me without reason maliciously wink the eye.

They do not speak peaceably, but devise false accusations.

O LORD, you have seen this; be not silent. Do not be far from me, O LORD.

Psalm 35:11-15,19,20,22

Even my close friend, whom I trusted, he who shared my bread, has lifted up his heel against me.

But you, O LORD, have mercy on me; raise me up, that I may repay them.

I know that you are pleased with me, for my enemy does not triumph over me.

Psalm 41:9-11

If an enemy were insulting me, I could endure it; if a foe were raising himself against me, I could hide from him.

But it is you, a man like myself, my companion, my close friend,

With whom I once enjoyed sweet fellowship as we walked with the throng at the house of God.

Psalm 55:12-14

He will cover you with his feathers, and under his wings you will find refuge; his faithfulness will be your shield and rampart.

You will not fear the terror of night, nor the arrow that flies by day.

Psalm 91:4,5

A truthful witness does not deceive, but a false witness pours out lies.

Proverbs 14:5

Because the Sovereign LORD helps me, I will not be disgraced. Therefore have I set my face like flint, and I know I will not be put to shame.

He who vindicates me is near. Who then will bring charges against me? Let us face each other! Who is my accuser? Let him confront me!

It is the Sovereign LORD who helps me. Who is he that will condemn me? They will all wear out like a garment; the moths will eat them up.

Isaiah 50:7-9

Do not gloat over me, my enemy! Though I have fallen, I will rise. Though I sit in darkness, the LORD will be my light.

Micah 7:8

Then one of the Twelve — the one called Judas Iscariot — went to the chief priests

And asked, "What are you willing to give me if I hand him over to you?" So they counted out for him thirty silver coins.

From then on Judas watched for an opportunity to hand him over.

Then he returned to the disciples and said to them, "Are you still sleeping and resting? Look, the hour is near, and the Son of Man is betrayed into the hands of sinners."

Matthew 26:14-16,45

Get rid of all bitterness, rage and anger, brawling and slander, along with every form of malice.

Ephesians 4:31

But the LORD stood at my side and gave me strength, so that through me the message might be fully proclaimed and all the Gentiles might hear it. And I was delivered from the lion's mouth.

2 Timothy 4:17

Keeping a clear conscience, so that those who speak maliciously against your good behavior in Christ may be ashamed of their slander.

1 Peter 3:16

...ır Business Depends
on You Alone

...g and courageous. Do not be
...errified because of them, for the
...ır God goes with you; he will never
lea... ...ou nor forsake you.

Deuteronomy 31:6

But as for you, be strong and do not give
up, for your work will be rewarded.

2 Chronicles 15:7

Be strong and take heart, all you who
hope in the LORD.

Psalm 31:24

I will instruct you and teach you in the
way you should go; I will counsel you and
watch over you.

Psalm 32:8

You guide me with your counsel, and
afterward you will take me into glory.

Psalm 73:24

Good will come to him who is generous
and lends freely, who conducts his affairs
with justice.

Psalm 112:5

For the LORD gives wisdom, and from his
mouth come knowledge and understanding.

Proverbs 2:6

Trust in the LORD with all your heart and
lean not on your own understanding.

Proverbs 3:5

Counsel and sound judgment are mine; I
have understanding and power.

Proverbs 8:14

Do you see a man skilled in his work?
He will serve before kings; he will not serve
before obscure men.

Proverbs 22:29

So do not fear, for I am with you; do not
be dismayed, for I am your God. I will
strengthen you and help you; I will uphold
you with my righteous right hand.

Isaiah 41:10

The Sovereign LORD is my strength; he
makes my feet like the feet of a deer, he
enables me to go on the heights. For the
director of music. On my stringed
instruments.

Habakkuk 3:19

But seek first his kingdom and his
righteousness, and all these things will be
given to you as well.

Matthew 6:33

And God is able to make all grace
abound to you, so that in all things at all

...g all that you need, you will
...very good work.

2 Corinthians 9:8

...to him who is able to do immea-
sura... more than all we ask or imagine,
according to his power that is at work within
us.

Ephesians 3:20

I can do everything through him who
gives me strength.

Philippians 4:13

So do not throw away your confidence;
it will be richly rewarded.

You need to persevere so that when you
have done the will of God, you will receive
what he has promised.

Hebrews 10:35,36

If any of you lacks wisdom, he should
ask God, who gives generously to all without
finding fault, and it will be given to him.

James 1:5

When Business Is Insufficient
To Continue Operations

But if from there you seek the LORD your
God, you will find him if you look for him
with all your heart and with all your soul.

Deuteronomy 4:29

Be strong and courageous. Do not be afraid or terrified because of them, for the LORD your God goes with you; he will never leave you nor forsake you.

Deuteronomy 31:6

Do not let this Book of the Law depart from your mouth; meditate on it day and night, so that you may be careful to do everything written in it. Then you will be prosperous and successful.

Have I not commanded you? Be strong and courageous. Do not be terrified; do not be discouraged, for the LORD your God will be with you wherever you go.

Joshua 1:8,9

David also said to Solomon his son, "Be strong and courageous, and do the work. Do not be afraid or discouraged, for the LORD God, my God, is with you. He will not fail you or forsake you until all the work for the service of the temple of the LORD is finished."

1 Chronicles 28:20

Teach me your way, O LORD; lead me in a straight path because of my oppressors.

Psalm 27:11

Since you are my rock and my fortress, for the sake of your name lead and guide me.

Psalm 31:3

For with you is the fountain of life; in your light we see light.

Psalm 36:9

When I am afraid, I will trust in you.

In God, whose word I praise, in God I trust; I will not be afraid. What can mortal man do to me?

Psalm 56:3,4

Even in darkness light dawns for the upright, for the gracious and compassionate and righteous man.

He will have no fear of bad news; his heart is steadfast, trusting in the LORD.

Psalm 112:4,7

It is better to take refuge in the LORD than to trust in man.

Psalm 118:8

Your word is a lamp to my feet and a light for my path.

Psalm 119:105

Trust in the LORD with all your heart and lean not on your own understanding.

Proverbs 3:5

The name of the LORD is a strong tower;
the righteous run to it and are safe.

Proverbs 18:10

No, in all these things we are more than
conquerors through him who loved us.

Romans 8:37

I can do everything through him who
gives me strength.

Philippians 4:13

But it is the spirit in a man, the breath of
the Almighty, that gives him understanding.

Job 32:8

I will praise the LORD, who counsels me;
even at night my heart instructs me.

Psalm 16:7

CHAPTER 10

THE BUSINESSWOMAN AND TIME-MANAGEMENT

Overcoming Disorganization

Show me your ways, O LORD, teach me your paths.

Psalm 25:4

I will instruct you and teach you in the way you should go; I will counsel you and watch over you.

Psalm 32:8

Cast your cares on the LORD and he will sustain you; he will never let the righteous fall.

Psalm 55:22

Trust in the LORD with all your heart and lean not on your own understanding;

In all your ways acknowledge him, and he will make your paths straight.

Proverbs 3:5,6

Make level paths for your feet and take only ways that are firm.

Proverbs 4:26

In his heart a man plans his course, but the LORD determines his steps.

Proverbs 16:9

Whether you turn to the right or to the left, your ears will hear a voice behind you, saying, "This is the way; walk in it."

Isaiah 30:21

He gives strength to the weary and increases the power of the weak.

Isaiah 40:29

Because the Sovereign LORD helps me, I will not be disgraced.

Isaiah 50:7a

I know, O LORD, that a man's life is not his own; it is not for man to direct his steps.

Jeremiah 10:23

Then, because so many people were coming and going that they did not even have a chance to eat, he [Jesus] said to them, "Come with me by yourselves to a quiet place and get some rest."

Mark 6:31

For God is not a God of disorder but of peace. As in all the congregations of the saints.

1 Corinthians 14:33

Therefore, my dear brothers, stand firm. Let nothing move you. Always give yourselves fully to the work of the LORD, because you know that your labor in the LORD is not in vain.

1 Corinthians 15:58

Let us not become weary in doing good, for at the proper time we will reap a harvest if we do not give up.

Galatians 6:9

Do not be anxious about anything, but in everything, by prayer and petition, with thanksgiving, present your requests to God.

And the peace of God, which transcends all understanding, will guard your hearts and your minds in Christ Jesus.

Philippians 4:6,7

For God did not give us a spirit of timidity, but a spirit of power, of love and of self-discipline.

2 Timothy 1:7

If any of you lacks wisdom, he should ask God, who gives generously to all without finding fault, and it will be given to him.

James 1:5

Working Through
an Overloaded Schedule

The LORD is a refuge for the oppressed, a stronghold in times of trouble.

Psalm 9:9

Cast your cares on the LORD and he will sustain you; he will never let the righteous fall.

Psalm 55:22

Unless the LORD had given me help, I would soon have dwelt in the silence of death.

When I said, "My foot is slipping," your love, O LORD, supported me.

Psalm 94:17,18

Great peace have they who love your law, and nothing can make them stumble.

Psalm 119:165

For your name's sake, O LORD, preserve my life; in your righteousness, bring me out of trouble.

Psalm 143:11

When you lie down, you will not be afraid; when you lie down, your sleep will be sweet.

Proverbs 3:24

But those who hope in the LORD will renew their strength. They will soar on wings like eagles; they will run and not grow weary, they will walk and not be faint.

Isaiah 40:31

Because the Sovereign LORD helps me, I will not be disgraced.

Isaiah 50:7a

I pray that out of his glorious riches he may strengthen you with power through his Spirit in your inner being.

Ephesians 3:16

Do not be anxious about anything, but in everything, by prayer and petition, with thanksgiving, present your requests to God.

And the peace of God, which transcends all understanding, will guard your hearts and your minds in Christ Jesus.

I can do everything through him who gives me strength.

Philippians 4:6,7,13

If any of you lacks wisdom, he should ask God, who gives generously to all without finding fault, and it will be given to him.

James 1:5

Do not cast me from your presence or take your Holy Spirit from me.

Restore to me the joy of your salvation and grant me a willing spirit, to sustain me.

Psalm 51:11,12

The Spirit of the LORD will rest on him — the Spirit of wisdom and of understanding, the Spirit of counsel and of power, the Spirit of knowledge and of the fear of the LORD.

Isaiah 11:2

For I will pour water on the thirsty land, and streams on the dry ground; I will pour out my Spirit on your offspring, and my blessing on your descendants.

They will spring up like grass in a meadow, like poplar trees by flowing streams.

Isaiah 44:3,4

But as for me, I am filled with power, with the Spirit of the LORD, and with justice and might, to declare to Jacob his transgression, to Israel his sin.

Micah 3:8

The Spirit gives life; the flesh counts for nothing. The words I have spoken to you are spirit and they are life.

John 6:63

The Spirit of truth. The world cannot accept him, because it neither sees him nor knows him. But you know him, for he lives with you and will be in you.

But the Counselor, the Holy Spirit, whom the Father will send in my name, will teach you all things and will remind you of everything I have said to you.

John 14:17,26

But when he, the Spirit of truth, comes, he will guide you into all truth. He will not speak on his own; he will speak only what he hears, and he will tell you what is yet to come.

John 16:13

In the same way, the Spirit helps us in our weakness. We do not know what we ought to pray for, but the Spirit himself intercedes for us with groans that words cannot express.

And he who searches our hearts knows the mind of the Spirit, because the Spirit intercedes for the saints in accordance with God's will.

Who shall separate us from the love of Christ? Shall trouble or hardship or persecution or famine or nakedness or danger or sword?

No, in all these things we are more than conquerors through him who loved us.

Romans 8:26,27,35,37

May the God of hope fill you with all joy and peace as you trust in him, so that you may overflow with hope by the power of the Holy Spirit.

Romans 15:13

Finally, be strong in the LORD and in his mighty power.

In addition to all this, take up the shield of faith, with which you can extinguish all the flaming arrows of the evil one.

And pray in the Spirit on all occasions with all kinds of prayers and requests. With this in mind, be alert and always keep on praying for all the saints.

Ephesians 6:10,16,18

But you, dear friends, build yourselves up in your most holy faith and pray in the Holy Spirit.

Jude 20

CHAPTER 11

THE BUSINESSWOMAN
AND HER FAMILY

Helping a Family Member Who Is Sick

The LORD will keep you free from every disease. He will not inflict on you the horrible diseases you knew in Egypt, but he will inflict them on all who hate you.

Deuteronomy 7:15

Praise the LORD, O my soul, and forget not all his benefits —

Who forgives all your sins and heals all your diseases.

Psalm 103:2,3

My son, pay attention to what I say; listen closely to my words.

Do not let them out of your sight, keep them within your heart;

133

For they are life to those who find them and health to a man's whole body.

Proverbs 4:20-22

Surely he took up our infirmities and carried our sorrows, yet we considered him stricken by God, smitten by him, and afflicted.

But he was pierced for our transgressions, he was crushed for our iniquities; the punishment that brought us peace was upon him, and by his wounds we are healed.

Isaiah 53:4,5

Heal me, O LORD, and I will be healed; save me and I will be saved, for you are the one I praise.

Jeremiah 17:14

"But I will restore you to health and heal your wounds," declares the LORD.

Jeremiah 30:17a

Jesus said to him, "I will go and heal him."

Matthew 8:7

Jesus Christ is the same yesterday and today and forever.

Hebrews 13:8

Is any one of you in trouble? He should pray. Is anyone happy? Let him sing songs of praise.

Is any one of you sick? He should call the elders of the church to pray over him and anoint him with oil in the name of the LORD.

And the prayer offered in faith will make the sick person well; the LORD will raise him up. If he has sinned, he will be forgiven.

Therefore confess your sins to each other and pray for each other so that you may be healed. The prayer of a righteous man is powerful and effective.

James 5:13-16

Dear friend, I pray that you may enjoy good health and that all may go well with you, even as your soul is getting along well.

3 John 2

Dealing With Insufficient Family Time

Only be careful, and watch yourselves closely so that you do not forget the things your eyes have seen or let them slip from your heart as long as you live. Teach them to your children and to their children after them.

Deuteronomy 4:9

These commandments that I give you today are to be upon your hearts.

Impress them on your children. Talk about them when you sit at home and when you walk along the road, when you lie down and when you get up.

Deuteronomy 6:6,7

Fix these words of mine in your hearts and minds; tie them as symbols on your hands and bind them on your foreheads.

Teach them to your children, talking about them when you sit at home and when you walk along the road, when you lie down and when you get up.

Deuteronomy 11:18,19

He decreed statutes for Jacob and established the law in Israel, which he commanded our forefathers to teach their children.

Psalm 78:5

So the next generation would know them, even the children yet to be born, and they in turn would tell their children.

Then they would put their trust in God and would not forget his deeds but would keep his commands.

Psalm 78:6,7

Teach us to number our days aright, that we may gain a heart of wisdom.

Psalm 90:12

Blessed are all who fear the LORD, who walk in his ways.

You will eat the fruit of your labor; blessings and prosperity will be yours.

Your wife will be like a fruitful vine within your house; your sons will be like olive shoots around your table.

Thus is the man blessed who fears the LORD.

Psalm 128:1-4

In his heart a man plans his course, but the LORD determines his steps.

Proverbs 16:9

The righteous man leads a blameless life; blessed are his children after him.

Proverbs 20:7

Train a child in the way he should go, and when he is old he will not turn from it.

Proverbs 22:6

The father of a righteous man has great joy; he who has a wise son delights in him.

Proverbs 23:24

By wisdom a house is built, and through understanding it is established.

Proverbs 24:3

Discipline your son, and he will give you peace; he will bring delight to your soul.

Proverbs 29:17

He will be the sure foundation for your times, a rich store of salvation and wisdom and knowledge; the fear of the LORD is the key to this treasure.

Isaiah 33:6

All your sons will be taught by the LORD, and great will be your children's peace.

In righteousness you will be established: Tyranny will be far from you; you will have nothing to fear. Terror will be far removed; it will not come near you.

Isaiah 54:13,14

Tell it to your children, and let your children tell it to their children, and their children to the next generation.

Joel 1:3

But seek first his kingdom and his righteousness, and all these things will be given to you as well.

Matthew 6:33

Be very careful, then, how you live —
not as unwise but as wise,

Making the most of every opportunity,
because the days are evil.

Ephesians 5:15,16

Fathers, do not exasperate your children;
instead, bring them up in the training and
instruction of the LORD.

Ephesians 6:4

Be wise in the way you act toward
outsiders; make the most of every opportunity.

Colossians 4:5

He must manage his own family well
and see that his children obey him with
proper respect.

If anyone does not know how to manage
his own family, how can he take care of
God's church?

1 Timothy 3:4,5

If anyone does not provide for his
relatives, and especially for his immediate
family, he has denied the faith and is worse
than an unbeliever.

1 Timothy 5:8

Facing Marital Problems

The LORD God said, "It is not good for the man to be alone. I will make a helper suitable for him."

For this reason a man will leave his father and mother and be united to his wife, and they will become one flesh.

Genesis 2:18,24

Hatred stirs up dissension, but love covers over all wrongs.

Proverbs 10:12

And provide for those who grieve in Zion — to bestow on them a crown of beauty instead of ashes, the oil of gladness instead of mourning, and a garment of praise instead of a spirit of despair. They will be called oaks of righteousness, a planting of the LORD for the display of his splendor.

Isaiah 61:3

For if you forgive men when they sin against you, your heavenly Father will also forgive you.

But if you do not forgive men their sins, your Father will not forgive your sins.

Matthew 6:14,15

Some Pharisees came and tested him by asking, "Is it lawful for a man to divorce his wife?"

"What did Moses command you?" he replied.

They said, "Moses permitted a man to write a certificate of divorce and send her away."

"It was because your hearts were hard that Moses wrote you this law," Jesus replied.

"But at the beginning of creation God 'made them male and female.'

"Therefore what God has joined together, let man not separate."

Mark 10:2-6,9

Do not deprive each other except by mutual consent and for a time, so that you may devote yourselves to prayer. Then come together again so that Satan will not tempt you because of your lack of self-control.

To the married I give this command (not I, but the LORD): A wife must not separate from her husband.

1 Corinthians 7:5,10

Love is patient, love is kind. It does not envy, it does not boast, it is not proud.

It always protects, always trusts, always hopes, always perseveres.

1 Corinthians 13:4,7

Submit to one another out of reverence for Christ.

Wives, submit to your husbands as to the LORD.

Husbands, love your wives, just as Christ loved the church and gave himself up for her.

In this same way, husbands ought to love their wives as their own bodies. He who loves his wife loves himself.

However, each one of you also must love his wife as he loves himself, and the wife must respect her husband.

Ephesians 5:21,22,25,28,33

Wives, submit to your husbands, as is fitting in the LORD.

Husbands, love your wives and do not be harsh with them.

Colossians 3:18,19

CHAPTER 12

THE BUSINESSWOMAN AND HER FINANCES

Good will come to him who is generous and lends freely, who conducts his affairs with justice.

Psalm 112:5

Lazy hands make a man poor, but diligent hands bring wealth.

Proverbs 10:4

Diligent hands will rule, but laziness ends in slave labor.

Proverbs 12:24

The sluggard craves and gets nothing, but the desires of the diligent are fully satisfied.

Proverbs 13:4

Do not love sleep or you will grow poor; stay awake and you will have food to spare.

Proverbs 20:13

Do you see a man skilled in his work? He will serve before kings; he will not serve before obscure men.

Proverbs 22:29

He who works his land will have abundant food, but the one who chases fantasies will have his fill of poverty.

Proverbs 28:19

But seek first his kingdom and his righteousness, and all these things will be given to you as well.

Matthew 6:33

Give, and it will be given to you. A good measure, pressed down, shaken together and running over, will be poured into your lap. For with the measure you use, it will be measured to you.

Luke 6:38

Never be lacking in zeal, but keep your spiritual fervor, serving the LORD.

Romans 12:11

Remember this: Whoever sows sparingly will also reap sparingly, and whoever sows generously will also reap generously.

2 Corinthians 9:6

And my God will meet all your needs according to his glorious riches in Christ Jesus.

Philippians 4:19

But remember the LORD your God, for it is he who gives you the ability to produce wealth, and so confirms his covenant, which he swore to your forefathers, as it is today.

Deuteronomy 8:18

Carefully follow the terms of this covenant, so that you may prosper in everything you do.

Deuteronomy 29:9

Be strong and very courageous. Be careful to obey all the law my servant Moses gave you; do not turn from it to the right or to the left, that you may be successful wherever you go.

Do not let this Book of the Law depart from your mouth; meditate on it day and night, so that you may be careful to do everything written in it. Then you will be prosperous and successful.

Joshua 1:7,8

I walk in the way of righteousness, along the paths of justice,

Bestowing wealth on those who love me and making their treasuries full.

Proverbs 8:20,21

The LORD will guide you always; he will satisfy your needs in a sun-scorched land and will strengthen your frame. You will be like a well-watered garden, like a spring whose waters never fail.

Isaiah 58:11

Dear friend, I pray that you may enjoy good health and that all may go well with you, even as your soul is getting along well.

3 John 2

May the favor of the LORD our God rest upon us; establish the work of our hands for us — yes, establish the work of our hands.

Psalm 90:17

Good will come to him who is generous and lends freely, who conducts his affairs with justice.

Surely he will never be shaken; a righteous man will be remembered forever.

He will have no fear of bad news; his heart is steadfast, trusting in the LORD.

His heart is secure, he will have no fear; in the end he will look in triumph on his foes.

Psalm 112:5-8

Commit to the LORD whatever you do, and your plans will succeed.

Proverbs 16:3

So do not worry, saying, "What shall we eat?" or "What shall we drink?" or "What shall we wear?"

For the pagans run after all these things, and your heavenly Father knows that you need them.

But seek first his kingdom and his righteousness, and all these things will be given to you as well.

Matthew 6:31-33

Be careful that you do not forget the LORD your God, failing to observe his commands, his laws and his decrees that I am giving you this day.

But remember the LORD your God, for it is he who gives you the ability to produce wealth, and so confirms his covenant, which he swore to your forefathers, as it is today.

Deuteronomy 8:11,18

He who walks righteously and speaks what is right, who rejects gain from extortion and keeps his hand from accepting bribes, who stops his ears against plots of murder and shuts his eyes against contemplating evil —

This is the man who will dwell on the heights, whose refuge will be the mountain fortress. His bread will be supplied, and water will not fail him.

Isaiah 33:15,16

He who has been stealing must steal no longer, but must work, doing something useful with his own hands, that he may have something to share with those in need.

Ephesians 4:28

But as for you, be strong and do not give up, for your work will be rewarded.

2 Chronicles 15:7

Make vows to the LORD your God and fulfill them; let all the neighboring lands bring gifts to the One to be feared.

Psalm 76:11

Good will come to him who is generous and lends freely, who conducts his affairs with justice.

He has scattered abroad his gifts to the poor, his righteousness endures forever; his horn will be lifted high in honor.

Psalm 112:5,9

Honor the LORD with your wealth, with the firstfruits of all your crops;

Then your barns will be filled to overflowing, and your vats will brim over with new wine.

Proverbs 3:9,10

Lazy hands make a man poor, but diligent hands bring wealth.

Proverbs 10:4

He who is kind to the poor lends to the LORD, and he will reward him for what he has done.

Proverbs 19:17

All day long he craves for more, but the righteous give without sparing.

Proverbs 21:26

A generous man will himself be blessed, for he shares his food with the poor.

Proverbs 22:9

He who gives to the poor will lack nothing, but he who closes his eyes to them receives many curses.

Proverbs 28:27

Cast your bread upon the waters, for after many days you will find it again.

Ecclesiastes 11:1

If you are willing and obedient, you will eat the best from the land.

Isaiah 1:19

"Bring the whole tithe into the storehouse, that there may be food in my house. Test me in this," says the LORD Almighty, "and see if I will not throw open the floodgates of heaven and pour out so much blessing that you will not have room enough for it.

I will prevent pests from devouring your crops, and the vines in your fields will not cast their fruit," says the LORD Almighty.

Malachi 3:10,11

Give to the one who asks you, and do not turn away from the one who wants to borrow from you.

Matthew 5:42

On the first day of every week, each one of you should set aside a sum of money in keeping with his income, saving it up, so that when I come no collections will have to be made.

1 Corinthians 16:2

Remember this: Whoever sows sparingly will also reap sparingly, and whoever sows generously will also reap generously.

Each man should give what he has decided in his heart to give, not reluctantly or under compulsion, for God loves a cheerful giver.

And God is able to make all grace abound to you, so that in all things at all times, having all that you need, you will abound in every good work.

2 Corinthians 9:6-8

Command those who are rich in this present world not to be arrogant nor to put their hope in wealth, which is so uncertain, but to put their hope in God, who richly provides us with everything for our enjoyment.

Command them to do good, to be rich in good deeds, and to be generous and willing to share.

In this way they will lay up treasure for themselves as a firm foundation for the coming age, so that they may take hold of the life that is truly life.

1 Timothy 6:17-19

If anyone has material possessions and sees his brother in need but has no pity on him, how can the love of God be in him?

Dear children, let us not love with words or tongue but with actions and in truth.

1 John 3:17,18

CHAPTER 13

THE BUSINESSWOMAN AND HER PERSONAL LIFE

Dealing With Stress

One of you routs a thousand, because the LORD your God fights for you, just as he promised.

Joshua 23:10

He will guard the feet of his saints, but the wicked will be silenced in darkness. "It is not by strength that one prevails."

I Samuel 2:9

This is what the LORD says to you: Do not be afraid or discouraged because of this vast army. For the battle is not yours, but God's.

2 Chronicles 20:15b

But you are a shield around me, O LORD; you bestow glory on me and lift up my head.

Psalm 3:3

In the morning, O LORD, you hear my voice; in the morning I lay my requests before you and wait in expectation.

Psalm 5:3

The LORD is a refuge for the oppressed, a stronghold in times of trouble.

Psalm 9:9

I love you, O LORD, my strength.

The LORD is my rock, my fortress and my deliverer; my God is my rock, in whom I take refuge. He is my shield and the horn of my salvation, my stronghold.

Psalm 18:1,2

Though an army besiege me, my heart will not fear; though war break out against me, even then will I be confident.

For in the day of trouble he will keep me safe in his dwelling; he will hide me in the shelter of his tabernacle and set me high upon a rock.

Psalm 27:3,5

My flesh and my heart may fail, but God is the strength of my heart and my portion forever.

Psalm 73:26

Praise the LORD, O my soul, and forget not all his benefits —

Who satisfies your desires with good things so that your youth is renewed like the eagles's.

Psalm 103:2,5

He sent forth his word and healed them; he rescued them from the grave.

Psalm 107:20

May there be peace within your walls and security within your citadels.

Psalm 122:7

In vain you rise early and stay up late, toiling for food to eat — for he grants sleep to those he loves.

Psalm 127:2

When you lie down, you will not be afraid; when you lie down, your sleep will be sweet.

Proverbs 3:24

Wicked men are overthrown and are no more, but the house of the righteous stand firm.

Provers 12:7

He who fears the LORD has a secure fortress, and for his children it will be a refuge.

Proverbs 14:26

He gives strength to the weary and increases the power of the weak.

But those who hope in the LORD will renew their strength. They will soar on wings like eagles; they will run and not grow weary, they will walk and not be faint.

Isaiah 40:29,31

So do not fear, for I am with you; do not be dismayed, for I am your God. I will strengthen you and help you; I will uphold you with my righteous right hand.

Isaiah 41:10

"Not by might nor by power, but by my Spirit," says the LORD Almighty.

Zechariah 4:6b

Do not let your hearts be troubled. Trust in God; trust also in me.

Peace I leave with you; my peace I give you. I do not give to you as the world gives. Do not let your hearts be troubled and do not be afraid.

John 14:1,27

Do not be anxious about anything, but in everything, by prayer and petition, with thanksgiving, present your requests to God.

And the peace of God, which transcends all understanding, will guard your hearts and your minds in Christ Jesus.

Philippians 4:6,7

Cast all your anxiety on him because he cares for you.

1 Peter 5:7

If this is so, then the Lord knows how to rescue godly men from trials and to hold the unrighteous for the day of judgment, while continuing their punishment.

2 Peter 2:9

Dealing With Being Overworked

I will lie down and sleep in peace, for you alone, O LORD, make me dwell in safety.

Psalm 4:8

He makes me lie down in green pastures, he leads me beside quiet waters,

He restores my soul. He guides me in paths of righteousness for his name's sake.

Psalm 23:2,3

The LORD gives strength to his people; the LORD blesses his people with peace.

Psalm 29:11

Delight yourself in the LORD and he will give you the desires of your heart.

Commit your way to the LORD; trust in him and he will do this:

Be still before the LORD and wait patiently for him; do not fret when men succeed in their ways, when they carry out their wicked schemes.

But the meek will inherit the land and enjoy great peace.

Psalm 37:4,5,7,11

My flesh and my heart may fail, but God is the strength of my heart and my portion forever.

Psalm 73:26

I will listen to what God the LORD will say; he promises peace to his people, his saints — but let them not return to folly.

Psalm 85:8

You will keep in perfect peace him whose mind is steadfast, because he trusts in you.

Isaiah 26:3

To whom he said, "This is the resting place, let the weary rest"; and, "This is the place of repose" — but they would not listen.

Isaiah 28:12

This is what the Sovereign LORD, the Holy One of Israel, says: "In repentance and rest is your salvation, in quietness and trust is your strength, but you would have none of it."

Isaiah 30:15

Come to me, all you who are weary and burdened, and I will give you rest.

Take my yoke upon you and learn from me, for I am gentle and humble in heart, and you will find rest for your souls.

Matthew 11:28,29

Then, because so many people were coming and going that they did not even have a chance to eat, he said to the, "Come with me by yourselves to a quiet place and get some rest."

Mark 6:31

Peace I leave with you; my peace I give you. I do not give to you as the world gives. Do not let your hearts be troubled and do not be afraid.

John 14:27

Facing Controversy

My lips will not speak wickedness, and my tongue will utter no deceit.

Job 27:4

Since you are my rock and my fortress, for the sake of your name lead and guide me.

Free me from the trap that is set for me, for you are my refuge.

Into your hands I commit my spirit; redeem me, O LORD, the God of truth.

Psalm 31:3-5

You are my hiding place; you will protect me from trouble and surround me with songs of deliverance. *Selah*

Psalm 32:7

Commit your way to the LORD; trust in him and he will do this;

He will make your righteousness shine like the dawn, the justice of your cause like the noonday sun.

Be still before the LORD and wait patiently for him; do not fret when men succeed in their ways, when they carry out their wicked schemes.

Psalm 37:5-7

I wait for you, O LORD; you will answer, O LORD my God.

Psalm 38:15

He who sacrifices thank offerings honors me, and he prepares the way so that I may show him the salvation of God.

Psalm 50:23

I call on the LORD in my distress, and he answers me.

Save me, O LORD, from lying lips and from deceitful tongues.

Psalm 120:1,2

Though I walk in the midst of trouble, you preserve my life; you stretch out your hand against the anger of my foes, with your right hand you save me.

Psalm 138:7

There are six things the LORD hates, seven that are detestable to him:

Haughty eyes, a lying tongue, hands that shed innocent blood,

A heart that devises wicked schemes, feet that are quick to rush into evil,

A false witness who pours out lies and a man who stirs up dissension among brothers.

Proverbs 6:16-19

Truthful lips endure forever, but a lying tongue lasts only a moment.

Proverbs 12:19

Do not say, "I'll do to him as he has done to me; I'll pay that man back for what he did."

Proverbs 24:29

When you pass through the waters, I will be with you; and when you pass through the rivers, they will not sweep over you. When you walk through the fire, you will not be burned; the flames will not set you ablaze.

Isaiah 43:2

The LORD will guide you always; he will satisfy your needs in a sun-scorched land and will strengthen your frame. You will be like a well-watered garden, like a spring whose waters never fail.

Isaiah 58:11

The LORD is good, a refuge in times of trouble. He cares for those who trust in him.

Nahum 1:7

And when you stand praying, if you hold anything against anyone, forgive him, so that your Father in heaven may forgive you your sins.

Mark 11:25

Who is going to harm you if you are eager to do good?

1 Peter 3:13

Cast all your anxiety on him because he cares for you.

1 Peter 5:7

Dealing With Feeling Threatened

After this, the word of the LORD came to Abram in a vision: "Do not be afraid, Abram. I am your shield, your very great reward"

Genesis 15:1

Blessed are you, O Israel! Who is like you, a people saved by the LORD? He is your shield and helper and your glorious sword. Your enemies will cower before you, and you will trample down their high place.

Deuteronomy 33:29

He said: "The LORD is my rock, my fortress and my deliverer."

2 Samuel 22:2

O LORD, how many are my foes! How many rise up against me!

Many are saying of me, "God will not deliver him: *Selah*

But you are a shield around me, O LORD; you bestow glory on me and lift up my head.

Psalm 3:1-3

In my distress I called to the LORD; I cried to my God for help. From his temple he heard my voice; my cry came before him, into his ears.

163

You give me your shield of victory, and your right hand sustains me; you stoop down to make me great.

Psalm 18:6,35

The LORD is my strength and my shield; my heart trusts in him, and I am helped. My heart leaps for joy and I will give thanks to him in song.

Psalm 28:7

The angle of the LORD encamps around those who fear him, and he delivers them.

Psalm 34:7

When I am afraid, I will trust in you.

In God, whose word I praise, in God I trust; I will not be afraid. What can mortal man do to me?

Psalm 56:3,4

For the LORD God is a sun and shield; the LORD bestows favor and honor; no good thing does he withhold from those whose walk is blameless.

Psalm 84:11

He will cover you with his feathers, and under his wings you will find refuge; his faithfulness will be your shield and rampart.

Psalm 91:4

You who fear him, trust in the LORD —
he is their help and shield.

Psalm 115:11

You are my refuge and my shield; I have
put my hope in your word.

Psalm 119:114

He is my loving God and my fortress,
my stronghold and my deliverer, my shield,
in whom I take refuge, who subdues peoples
under me.

Psalm 144:2

So do not fear, for I am with you; do not
be dismayed, for I am your God. I will
strengthen you and help you; I will uphold
you with my righteous right hand.

For I am the LORD, your God, who takes
hold of your right hand and says to you, Do
not fear; I will help you.

Isaiah 41:10,13

In addition to all this, take up the shield
of faith, with which you can extinguish all
the flaming arrows of the evil one.

Ephesians 6:16

Dealing With Depression

For his anger lasts only a moment, but
his favor lasts a lifetime; weeping may

remain for a night, but rejoicing comes in the morning.

Psalm 30:5

But the eyes of the LORD are on those who fear him, on those whose hope is in his unfailing love.

Psalm 33:18

The righteous cry out, and the LORD hears them; he delivers them from all their troubles.

Psalm 34:17

On my bed I remember you; I think of you through the watches of the night.

Psalm 63:6

I will praise you, O LORD, with all my heart; before the "gods" I will sing your praise.

Psalm 138:1

He heals the brokenhearted and binds up their wounds.

Psalm 147:3

Blessed is the man who finds wisdom, the man who gains understanding,

Her ways are pleasant ways, and all her paths are peace.

She is a tree of life to those who embrace her; those who lay hold of her will be blessed.

Proverbs 3:13,17,18

The desert and the parched land will be glad; the wilderness will rejoice and blossom. Like the crocus,

And the ransomed of the LORD will return. They will enter Zion with singing; everlasting joy will crown their hands. Gladness and joy will overtake them, and sorrow and sighing will flee away.

Isaiah 35:1,10

But those who hope in the LORD will renew their strength. They will soar on wings like eagles; they will run and not grow weary, they will walk and not be faint.

Isaiah 40:31

So do not fear, for I am with you; do not be dismayed, for I am your God. I will strengthen you and help you; I will uphold you with my righteous right hand.

Isaiah 41:10

When you pass through the waters, I will be with you; and when you pass through the rivers, they will not sweep over you. When you walk through the fire, you will not be burned; the flames will not set you ablaze.

Isaiah 43:2

And provide for those who grieve in Zion — to bestow on them a crown of beauty instead of ashes, the oil of gladness instead of mourning, and a garment of praise instead of a spirit of despair. They will be called oaks of righteousness, a planting of the LORD for the display of his splendor.

Isaiah 61:3

For I am convinced that neither death nor life, neither angels nor demons, neither the present nor the future, nor any powers,

Neither height nor depth, nor anything else in all creation, will be able to separate us from the love of God that is in Christ Jesus our Lord.

Romans 8:38,39

Praise be to the God and Father of our LORD Jesus Christ, the Father of compassion and the God of all comfort,

Who comforts us in all our troubles, so that we can comfort those in any trouble with the comfort we ourselves have received from God.

2 Corinthians 1:3,4

Dear friends, do not be surprised at the painful trial you are suffering, as though something strange were happening to you.

But rejoice that you participate in the sufferings of Christ, so that you may be overjoyed when his glory is revealed.

1 Peter 4:12,13

Overcoming Feeling Lonely

The eternal God is your refuge, and underneath are the everlasting arms. He will drive out your enemy before you, saying, "Destroy him!"

Deuteronomy 33:27

For the sake of his great name the LORD will not reject his people, because the LORD was pleased to make you his own.

1 Samuel 12:22

Those who know your name will trust in you, for you, LORD, have never forsaken those who seek you.

Psalm 9:10

Even though I walk through the valley of the shadow of death, I will fear no evil, for you are with me; your rod and your staff, they comfort me.

Psalm 23:4

Though my father and mother forsake me, the LORD will receive me.

Psalm 27:10

I was young and now I am old, yet I have never seen the righteous forsaken or their children begging bread.

For the LORD loves the just and will not forsake his faithful ones. They will be protected forever, but the offspring of the wicked will be cut off.

Psalm 37:25,28

God is our refuge and strength, an ever-present help in trouble.

Psalm 46:1

He heals the brokenhearted and binds up their wounds.

Psalm 147:3

You have been a refuge for the poor, a refuge for the needy in his distress, a shelter from the storm and a shade from the heat. For the breath of the ruthless is like a storm driving against a wall.

Isaiah 25:4

He gives strength to the weary and increases the power of the weak.

Isaiah 40:29

So do not fear, for I am with you; do not be dismayed, for I am your God. I will strengthen you and help you; I will uphold you with my righteous right hand.

Isaiah 41:10

"Though the mountains be shaken and the hills be removed, yet my unfailing love for you will not be shaken, nor my covenant of peace be removed," says the LORD, who has compassion on you.

Isaiah 54:10

And even the very hairs of your head are all numbered.

Matthew 10:30

And teaching them to obey everything I have commanded you. And surely I am with you always, to the very end of the age.

Matthew 28:20

Do not let your hearts be troubled. Trust in God; trust also in me.

And I will ask the Father, and he will give you another Counselor to be with you forever —

The Spirit of truth. The world cannot accept him, because it neither sees him nor knows him. But you know him, for he lives with you and will be in you.

I will not leave you as orphans; I will come to you.

John 14:1, 16-18

The LORD will rescue me from every evil attack and will bring me safely to his heavenly kingdom. To him be glory for ever and ever. Amen.

2 Timothy 4:18

For we do not have a high priest who is unable to sympathize with our weaknesses, but we have one who has been tempted in every way, just as we are — yet was without sin.

Let us then approach the throne of grace with confidence, so that we may receive mercy and find grace to help us in our time of need.

Hebrews 4:15,16

Keep your lives free from the love of money and be content with what you have, because God has said, "Never will I leave you; never will I forsake you."

Hebrews 13:5

Cast all your anxiety on him because he cares for you.

1 Peter 5:7

Avoiding the Temptation To Quit

Be strong and courageous, because you will lead these people to inherit the land I swore to their forefathers to give them.

Joshua 1:6

But the men of Israel encouraged one another and again took up their positions where they had stationed themselves the first day.

Judges 20:22

David was greatly distressed because the men were talking of stoning him; each one was bitter in spirit because of his sons and daughters. But David found strength in the LORD his God.

1 Samuel 30:6

Wait for the LORD; be strong and take heart and wait for the LORD.

Psalm 27:14

Be strong and take heart, all you who hope in the LORD.

Psalm 31:24

I wait for you, O LORD; you will answer, O LORD my God.

Psalm 38:15

But now, LORD, what do I look for? My hope is in you.

Psalm 39:7

Through you we push back our enemies; through your name we trample our foes.

Psalm 44:5

But as for me, I will always have hope; I will praise you more and more.

Psalm 71:14

Blessed is he whose help is the God of Jacob, whose hope is in the LORD his God.

Psalm 146:5

Know that the LORD is God. It is he who made us, and we are his; we are his people, the sheep of his pasture.

Psalm 100:3

I lift up my eyes to you, to you whose throne is in heaven.

As the eyes of slaves look to the hand of their master, as the eyes of a maid look to the hand of her mistress, so our eyes look to the LORD our God, till he shows us his mercy.

Psalm 123:1,2

Trust in the LORD with all your heart and lean not on your own understanding.

Proverbs 3:5

"'If you can'?" said Jesus. "Everything is possible for him who believes."

Immediately the boy's father exclaimed, "I do believe; help me overcome my unbelief!"

Mark 9:23,24

Therefore I tell you, whatever you ask for in prayer, believe that you have received it, and it will be yours.

Mark 11:24

But if we hope for what we do not yet have, we wait for it patiently.

Who shall separate us from the love of Christ? Shall trouble or hardship or persecution or famine or nakedness or danger or sword?

As it is written: "For your sake we face death all day long; we are considered as sheep to be slaughtered."

No, in all these things we are more than conquerors through him who loved us.

For I am convinced that neither death nor life, neither angels nor demons, neither the present nor the future, nor any powers,

Neither heights nor depth, nor anything else in all creation, will be able to separate us from the love of God that is in Christ Jesus our LORD.

Romans 8:25,35,36-39

I can do everything through him who gives me strength.

Philippians 4:13

Being strengthened with all power according to his glorious might so that you may have great endurance and patience and joyfully.

Colossians 1:11,12

Now faith is being sure of what we hope for and certain of what we do not see.

Hebrews 11:1

You, dear children, are from God and have overcome them, because the one who is in you is greater than the one who is in the world.

I John 4:4

Finding Encouragement

When I called, you answered me; you made me bold and stouthearted.

Psalm 138:3

Though I walk in the midst of trouble, you preserve my life; you stretch out your hand against the anger of my foes, with your right hand you save me.

The LORD will fulfill [his purpose] for me; your love, O LORD endures forever — do not abandon the works of your hands.

Psalm 138: 7,8

But you, O LORD, have mercy on me; raise me up, that I may repay them.

Psalm 41:10

When you pass through the waters, I will be with you; and when you pass through the rivers, they will not sweep over you. When you walk through the fire, you will not be burned; the flames will not set you ablaze.

Isaiah 43:2

The LORD will surely comfort Zion and will look with compassion on all her ruins; he will make her deserts like Eden, her wastelands like the garden of the LORD. Joy and gladness will be found in her, thanksgiving and the sound of singing.

Isaiah 51:3

I, even I, am he who comforts you. Who are you that you fear mortal men, the sons of men, who are but grass.

Isaiah 51:12

The LORD will fulfill [his purpose] for me; your love, O LORD, endures forever — do not abandon the works of your hands.

Psalm 138:8

"For I know the plans I have for you," declares the LORD, plans to prosper you and not to harm you, plans to give you hope and a future."

Jeremiah 29:11

May our LORD Jesus Christ himself and God our Father, who loves us and by his grace gave us eternal encouragement and good hope,

Encourage your hearts and strengthen you in every good deed and word.

2 Thessalonians 2:16,17

God is not unjust; he will not forget your work and the love you have shown him as you have helped his people and continue to help them.

We want each of you to show this same diligence to the very end, in order to make your hope sure.

We do not want you to become lazy, but to imitate those who through faith and patience inherit what has been promised.

Hebrews 6:10-12

But from everlasting to everlasting the LORD'S love is with those who fear him, and his righteousness with their children's children.

Psalm 103:17

Be strong and courageous. Do not be afraid or terrified because of them, for the LORD your God goes with you; he will never leave you nor forsake you.

Deuteronomy 31:6

Yet I am always with you; you hold me by my right hand.

Psalm 73:23

Have I not commanded you? Be strong and courageous. Do not be terrified; do not be discouraged, for the LORD your God will be with you wherever you go.

Joshua 1:9

So he said to me, "This is the word of the LORD to Zerubbabel: 'Not by might nor by power, but by my Spirit,' says the LORD Almighty."

Zechariah 4:6

Trust in the LORD and do good; dwell in the land and enjoy safe pasture.

Delight yourself in the LORD and he will give you the desires of your heart.

Commit your way to the LORD; trust in him and he will do this.

Psalm 37:3-5

Praise our God, O peoples, let the sound of his praise be heard;

He has preserved our lives and kept our feet from slipping.

Psalm 66:8,9

But thanks be to God, who always leads us in triumphal procession in Christ and through us spreads everywhere the fragrance of the knowledge of him.

2 Corinthians 2:14

I will praise God's name in song and glorify him with thanksgiving.

Psalm 69:30

The poor will see and be glad — you who seek God, may your hearts live!

Psalm 69:32

Being confident of this, that he who began a good work in you will carry it on to completion until the day of Christ Jesus.

Philippians 1:6

The path of the righteous is like the first gleam of dawn, shining ever brighter till the full light of day.

Proverbs 4:18

Facing the Need To Forgive

A man's wisdom gives him patience; it is to his glory to overlook an offense.

Proverbs 19:11

Do not gloat when your enemy falls; when he stumbles, do not let your heart rejoice,

Do not say, "I'll do to him as he has done to me; I'll pay that man back for what he did."

Proverbs 24:17, 29

If your enemy is hungry, give him food to eat; if he is thirsty, give him water to drink.

Proverbs 25:21

Blessed are the merciful, for they will be shown mercy.

Matthew 5:7

But I tell you, Do not resist an evil person. If someone strikes you on the right cheek, turn to him the other also.

Matthew 5:39

But I tell you: Love your enemies and pray for those who persecute you.

Matthew 5:44

Forgive us our debts, as we also have forgiven our debtors.

For if you forgive men when they sin against you, your heavenly Father will also forgive you.

But if you do not forgive men their sins, your Father will not forgive your sins.

Matthew 6:12,14,15

Then Peter came to Jesus and asked, "LORD, how many times shall I forgive my brother when he sins against me? Up to seven times?"

Matthew 18:21

Jesus answered, "I tell you, not seven times, but seventy-seven times."

Matthew 18:22

And when you stand praying, if you hold anything against anyone, forgive him, so that your Father in heaven may forgive you your sins.

Mark 11:25

So watch yourselves. "If your brother sins, rebuke him, and if he repents, forgive him.

"If he sins against you seven times in a day, and seven times comes back to you and says, 'I repent,' forgive him."

Luke 17:3,4

Bless those who persecute you; bless and do not curse.

Do not be overcome by evil, but overcome evil with good.

Romans 12:14,21

Be kind and compassionate to one another, forgiving each other, just as in Christ God forgave you.

Ephesians 4:32

Bear with each other and forgive whatever grievances you may have against one another. Forgive as the LORD forgave you.

Colossians 3:13

Do not repay evil with evil or insult with insult, but with blessing, because to this you were called so that you may inherit a blessing.

1 Peter 3:9

Finding Comfort

And I will ask the Father, and he will give you another counselor to be with you forever —

The Spirit of truth. The world cannot accept him, because it neither sees him nor knows him. But you know him, for he lives with you and will be in you.

I will not leave you as orphans; I will come to you.

John 14:16-18

But the Counselor, the Holy Spirit, whom the Father will send in my name, will teach you all things and will remind you of everything I have said to you.

John 14:26

But I tell you the truth: It is for your good that I am going away. Unless I go away, the counselor will not come to you; but if I go, I will send him to you.

John 16:7

Praise be to the God and Father of our LORD Jesus Christ, the Father of compassion and the God of all comfort,

Who comforts us in all our troubles, so that we can comfort those in any trouble with the comfort we ourselves have received from God.

For just as the sufferings of Christ flow over into our lives, so also through Christ our comfort overflows.

2 Corinthians 1:3-5

For anyone who speaks in a tongue does not speak to men but to God. Indeed, no one understands him; he utters mysteries with his spirit.

But everyone who prophesies speaks to men for their strengthening, encouragement and comfort.

1 Corinthians 14:2,3

Therefore encourage one another and build each other up, just as in fact you are doing.

1 Thessalonians 5:11

But you, dear friends, build yourselves up in your most holy faith and pray in the Holy Spirit.

Jude 20

David was greatly distressed because the men were talking of stoning him; each one was bitter in spirit because of his sons and daughters. But David found strength in the LORD his God.

1 Samuel 30:6

The eternal God is your refuge, and underneath are the everlasting arms. He will drive out your enemy before you, saying, "Destroy him!"

Deuteronomy 33:27

Even though I walk through the valley of the shadow of death, I will fear no evil, for you are with me; your rod and your staff, they comfort me.

Psalm 23:4

For in the day of trouble he will keep me safe in his dwelling; he will hide me in the shelter of his tabernacle and set me high upon a rock.

Then my head will be exalted above the enemies who surround me; at his tabernacle will I sacrifice with shouts of joy; I will sing and make music to the LORD.

Psalm 27:5,6

For his anger lasts only a moment, but his favor lasts a lifetime; weeping may remain for a night, but rejoicing comes in the morning.

Psalm 30:5

I will be glad and rejoice in your love, for you saw my affliction and knew the anguish of my soul.

Psalm 31:7

Cast your cares on the LORD and he will sustain you; he will never let the righteous fall.

Psalm 55:22

Record my lament; list my tears on your scroll — are they not in your record?

Then my enemies will turn back when I call for help. By this I will know that God is for me.

In God, whose word I praise, in the LORD, whose word I praise.

Psalm 56:8-10

My comfort in my suffering is this: Your promise preserves my life.

Psalm 119:50

I remember your ancient laws, O LORD, and I find comfort in them.

Psalm 119:52

Your decrees are the theme of my song wherever I lodge.

Psalm 119:54

Finding Faith When You Need It

But what does it say? "The word is near you; it is in your mouth and in your heart," that is, the word of faith we are proclaiming.

Romans 10:8

Consequently, faith comes from hearing the message, and the message is heard through the word of Christ.

Romans 10:17

As for God, his way is perfect; the word of the LORD is flawless. He is a shield for all who take refuge in him.

2 Samuel 22:31

The LORD is a refuge for the oppressed, a stronghold in times of trouble.

Those who know your name will trust in you, for you, LORD have never forsaken those who seek you.

Psalm 9:9,10

It is better to take refuge in the LORD than to trust in man.

It is better to take refuge in the LORD than to trust in princes.

Psalm 118:8,9

Those who trust in the LORD are like Mount Zion, which cannot be shaken but endures forever.

Psalm 125:1

My help comes from the LORD, the Maker of heaven and earth.

He will not let your foot slip — he who watches over you will not slumber;

Indeed, he who watches over Israel will neither slumber nor sleep.

Psalm 121:2-4

But let all who take refuge in you be glad; let them ever sing for joy. Spread your protection over them, that those who love your name may rejoice in you.

Psalm 5:11

May the God of hope fill you with all joy and peace as you trust in him, so that you may overflow with hope by the power of the Holy Spirit.

Romans 15:13

And we also thank God continually because, when you received the word of God, which you heard from us, you accepted it not as the word of men, but as it actually is, the word of God, which is at work in you who believe.

1 Thessalonians 2:13

But my righteous one will live by faith. And if he shrinks back, I will not be pleased with him.

But we are not of those who shrink back and are destroyed, but of those who believe and are saved.

Hebrews 10:38,39

For everyone born of God overcomes the world. This is the victory that has overcome the world, even our faith.

1 John 5:4

The LORD himself goes before you and will be with you; he will never leave you nor forsake you. Do not be afraid; do not be discouraged.

Deuteronomy 31:8

Early in the morning they left for the Desert of Tekoa. As they set out, Jehoshaphat stood and said, "Listen to me, Judah and people of Jerusalem! Have faith in the LORD your God and you will be upheld; have faith in his prophets and you will be successful."

2 Chronicles 20:20

Be strong and courageous. Do not be afraid or discouraged because of the king of Assyria and the vast army with him, for there is a greater power with us than with him.

With him is only the arm of flesh, but with us is the LORD our God to help us and to fight our battles. And the people gained confidence from what Hezekiah the king of Judah said.

2 Chronicles 32:7,8

Be not afraid, O land; be glad and rejoice. Surely the LORD has done great things.

Joel 2:21

See, he is puffed up; his desires are not upright — but the righteous will live by his faith.

Habakkuk 2:4

David also said to Solomon his son, "Be strong and courageous, and do the work. Do not be afraid or discouraged, for the LORD God, my God, is with you. We will not fail you or forsake you until all the work for the service of the temple of the LORD is finished."

1 Chronicles 28:20

The LORD is my shepherd, I shall not be in want.

Psalm 23:1

Finding Joy

You have made known to me the path of life; you will fill me with joy in your presence, with eternal pleasures at your right hand.

Psalm 16:11

Splendor and majesty are before him; strength and joy in his dwelling place.

1 Chronicles 16:27

And on that day they offered great sacrifices rejoicing because God had given them great joy. The women and children also rejoiced. The sound of rejoicing in Jerusalem could be heard far away.

Nehemiah 12:43

You have filled my heart with greater joy than when their grain and new wine abound.

Psalm 4:7

I will be glad and rejoice in you; I will sing praise to your name, O Most High.

Psalm 9:2

The precepts of the LORD are right, giving joy to the heart. The commands of the LORD are radiant, giving light to the eyes.

Psalm 19:8

The LORD is my strength and my shield; my heart trusts in him, and I am helped. My heart leaps for joy and I will give thanks to him in song.

Psalm 28:7

Then my soul will rejoice in the LORD and delight in his salvation.

Psalm 35:9

Will you not revive us again, that your people may rejoice in you?

Psalm 85:6

Blessed are those who have learned to acclaim you, who walk in the light of your presence, O LORD.

They rejoice in your name all day long; they exult in your righteousness.

Psalm 89:15,16

Shout for joy to the LORD, all the earth.

Worship the LORD with gladness; come before him with joyful songs.

Psalm 100:1,2

When the LORD brought back to the captives to Zion, we were like men who dreamed.

Our mouths were filled with laughter, our tongues with songs of joy. Then it was said among the nations, "The LORD has done great things for them."

Psalm 126:1,2

When your words came, I ate them; they were my joy and my heart's delight, for I bear your name, O LORD God almighty.

Jeremiah 15:16

However, do not rejoice that the spirits submit to you, but rejoice that your names are written in heaven.

Luke 10:20

I have told you this so that my joy may be in you and that your joy may be complete.

John 15:11

You have made known to me the paths of life; you will fill me with joy in your presence.

Acts 2:28

And the disciples were filled with joy and with the Holy Spirit.

Acts 13:52

For the kingdom of God is not a matter of eating and drinking, but of righteousness, peace and joy in the Holy Spirit.

Romans 14:17

For you were once darkness, but now you are light in the LORD. Live as children of light.

Ephesians 5:8

Whatever you have learned or received or heard from me, or seen in me — put it into practice. And the God of peace will be with you.

Philippians 4:9

Though you have not seen him, you love him; and even though you do not see him now, you believe in him and are filled with an inexpressible and glorious joy.

1 Peter 1:8

Finding Love When You Really Need It

And hope does not disappoint us, because God has poured out his love into our hearts by the Holy Spirit, whom he has given us.

Romans 5:5

And this is my prayer: that your love may abound more and more in knowledge and depth of insight,

So that you may be able to discern what is best and may be pure and blameless until the day of Christ,

Filled with the fruit of righteousness that comes through Jesus Christ — to the glory and praise of God.

Philippians 1:9-11

May the LORD make your love increase and overflow for each other and for everyone else, just as ours does for you.

May he strengthen your hearts so that you will be blameless and holy in the presence of our God and Father when our LORD Jesus comes with all his holy ones.

1 Thessalonians 3:12,13

Now about brotherly love we do not need to write to you, for you yourselves have been taught by God to love each other.

And in fact, you do love all the brothers throughout Macedonia. Yet we urge you, brothers, to do so more and more.

1 Thessalonians 4:9,10

May the LORD direct your hearts into God's love and Christ's perseverance.

2 Thessalonians 3:5

This is love: not that we loved God, but that he loved us and sent his Son as an atoning sacrifice for our sins.

Dear friends, since God so loved us, we also ought to love one another.

No one has ever seen God; but if we love one another, God lives in us and his love is made complete in us.

1 John 4:10-12

And so we know and rely on the love God has for us. God is love. Whoever lives in love lives in God, and God in him.

In this way, love is made complete among us so that we will have confidence on the day of judgment, because in this world we are like him.

There is no fear in love. But perfect love drives out fear, because fear has to do with punishment. The one who fears is not made perfect in love.

1 John 4:16-18

Hatred stirs up dissension, but love covers over all wrongs.

Proverbs 10:12

Place me like a seal over your heat, like a seal on your arm; for love is as strong as death, its jealously unyielding as the grave. It burns like blazing fire, like a mighty flame.

Many waters cannot quench love; rivers cannot wash it away. If one were to give all the wealth of his house for love, it would be utterly scorned.

Song of Songs 8:6,7

A friend loves at all times, and a brother is born for adversity.

Proverbs 17:17

Honor your father and mother, and love your neighbor as yourself.

Matthew 19:19

Love the LORD your God with all your heart and with all your soul and with all your strength.

Deuteronomy 6:5

And now, O Israel, what does the LORD your God ask of you but to fear the LORD your God, to walk in all his ways, to love him, to serve the LORD your God with all your heart and with all your soul.

Deuteronomy 10:12

But be very careful to keep the commandment and the law that Moses the servant of the LORD gave you: to love the LORD your God, to walk in all his ways, to obey his commands, to hold fast to him and to serve him with all your heart and all your soul.

Joshua 22:5

I love the LORD, for he heard my voice; he heard my cry for mercy.

Psalm 116:1

A new command I give you: Love one another. As I have loved you, so you must love one another.

By this all men will know that you are my disciples, if you love one another.

John 13:34,35

Now about food sacrificed to idols: We know that we all possess knowledge. Knowledge puffs up, but love builds up.

1 Corinthians 8:1

The goal of this command is love, which comes from a pure heart and a good conscience and a sincere faith.

1 Timothy 1:5

Above all, love each other deeply, because love covers over a multitude of sins.

1 Peter 4:8

Whoever loves his brother lives in the light, and there is nothing in him to make him stumble.

1 John 2:10

Finding Patience When You Need It

Be still before the LORD and wait patiently for him; do not fret when men succeed in their ways, when they carry out their wicked schemes.

Refrain from anger and turn from wrath; do not fret — it leads only to evil.

For evil men will be cut off, but those who hope in the LORD will inherit the land.

Psalm 37:7-9

The end of a matter is better than its beginning, and patience is better than pride.

Do not be quickly provoked in your spirit, for anger resides in the lap of fools.

Ecclesiastes 7:8,9

By standing firm you will gain life.

Luke 21:19

Not only so, but we also rejoice in our sufferings, because we know that suffering produces perseverance.

Romans 5:3

Let us not become weary in doing good, for at the proper time we will reap a harvest if we do not give up.

Galatians 6:9

As a prisoner for the LORD, then, I urge you to live a life worthy of the calling you have received.

Ephesians 4:1

Be completely humble and gentle; be patient, bearing with one another in love.

Ephesians 4:2

And we pray this in order that you may live a life worthy of the LORD and may please him in every way: bearing fruit in every good work, growing in the knowledge of God.

Being strengthened with all power according to his glorious might so that you may have great endurance and patience, and joyfully giving thanks to the Father, who has qualified you to share in the inheritance of the saints in the kingdom of light.

Colossians 1:10-12

And we urge you, brother, warn those who are idle, encourage the timid, help the weak, be patient with everyone.

1 Thessalonians 5:14

For this reason, when I could stand it no longer, I sent to find out about your faith. I was afraid that in some way the tempter might have tempted you and our efforts might have been useless.

1 Thessalonians 3:5

But you, man of God, flee from all this, and pursue righteousness, godliness, faith, love, endurance and gentleness.

1 Timothy 6:11

We do not want you to become lazy, but to imitate those who through faith and patience inherit what has been promised.

Hebrews 6:12

And so after waiting patiently, Abraham received what was promised.

Hebrews 6:15

You need to persevere so that when you have done the will of God, you will receive what he has promised.

Hebrews 10:36

Therefore, since we are surrounded by such a great cloud of witnesses, let us throw off everything that hinders and the sin that so easily entangles, and let us run with perseverance the race marked out for us.

Hebrews 12:1

Because you know that the testing of your faith develops perseverance.

Perseverance must finish its work so that you may be mature and complete, not lacking anything.

James 1:3,4

My dear brothers, take note of this:
Everyone should be quick to listen, slow to
speak and slow to become angry.

James 1:19

Be patient, then, brothers, until the
LORD'S coming. See how the farmer waits for
the land to yield its valuable crop and how
patient he is for the autumn and spring rains.

You too, be patient and stand firm,
because the LORD'S coming is near.

James 5:7,8

For this very reason, make every effort
to add to your faith goodness; and to
goodness, knowledge;

And to knowledge, self-control; and to
self-control, perseverance; and to perseverance, godliness.

2 Peter 1:5,6

This calls for patient endurance on the
part of the saints who obey God's commandments and remain faithful to Jesus.

Revelation 14:12

The Lord is not slow in keeping his
promise, as some understand slowness. He
is patient with you, not wanting anyone to
perish, but everyone to come to repentance.

2 Peter 3:9

Finding Peace

When a man's ways are pleasing to the LORD, he makes even his enemies live at peace with him.

Proverbs 16:7

It is to a man's honor to avoid strife, but every fool is quick to quarrel.

Proverbs 20:3

Also, seek the peace and prosperity of the city to which I have carried you into exile. Pray to the LORD for it, because if it prospers, you too will prosper.

Jeremiah 29:7

Blessed are the peacemakers, for they will be called sons of God.

Matthew 5:9

Submit to God and be at peace with him; in this way prosperity will come to you.

Job 22:21

But if he remains silent, who can condemn him? Yet he is over man and nation alike.

Job 34:29

You will keep in perfect peace him whose mind is steadfast, because he trusts in you.

Trust in the LORD forever, for the LORD, the LORD, is the rock eternal.

Isaiah 26:3,4

LORD, you establish peace for us; all that we have accomplished you have done for us.

Isaiah 26:12

Who, then, is the man that fears the LORD? He will instruct him in the way chosen for him.

He will spend his days in prosperity, and his descendants will inherit the land.

Psalm 25:12,13

Consider the blameless, observe the upright, there is a future for the man of peace.

Psalm 37:37

I will listen to what God the LORD will say; he promises peace to his people, his saints — but let them not return to folly.

Psalm 85:8

Great peace have they who love your law, and nothing can make them stumble.

Psalm 119:165

Those who trust in the LORD are like Mount Zion, which cannot be shaken but endures forever.

Psalm 125:1

Finding Peace

To whom he said, "This is the resting place, let the weary rest"; and, "This is the place of repose" — but they would not listen.

Isaiah 28:12

"The glory of this present house will be greater than the glory of the former house," says the LORD Almighty. "And in this place I will grant peace," declares the LORD Almighty.

Haggai 2:9

My covenant was with him, a covenant of life and peace, and I gave them to him; this called for reverence and he revered me and stood in awe of my name.

Malachi 2:5

To shine on those living in darkness and in the shadow of death, to guide our feet into the path of peace.

Luke 1:79

Peace I leave with you; my peace I give you.

I do not give to you as the world gives. Do not let your hearts be troubled and do not be afraid.

John 14:27

Therefore, since we have been justified through faith, we have peace with God through our LORD Jesus Christ.

Romans 5:1

For the kingdom of God is not a matter of eating and drinking, but of righteousness, peace and joy in the Holy Spirit.

Romans 14:17

Do not be anxious about anything, but in everything, by prayer and petition, with thanksgiving, present your requests to God.

And the peace of God, which transcends all understanding, will guard your hearts and your minds in Christ Jesus.

Philippians 4:6,7

Let the peace of Christ rule in your hearts, since as members of one body you were called to peace. And be thankful.

Colossians 3:15

Now may the LORD of peace himself give you peace at all times and in every way. The LORD be with all of you.

2 Thessalonians 3:16

He ransoms me unharmed from the battle waged against me, even though many oppose me.

Psalm 55:18

Finding Strength

The LORD is my strength and my song; he has become my salvation. He is my God, and I will praise him, my father's God, and I will exalt him.

Exodus 15:2

All his laws are before me; I have not turned away from his decrees.

2 Samuel 22:23

The LORD is my strength and my song; he has become my salvation.

Psalm 118:14

Surely God is my salvation; I will trust and not be afraid. the LORD, the LORD, is my strength and my song; he has become my salvation.

Isaiah 12:2

You armed me with strength for battle; you made my adversaries bow at my feet.

2 Samuel 22:40

It is God who arms me with strength and makes my way perfect.

Psalm 18:32

You armed me with strength for battle; you made my adversaries bow at my feet.

Psalm 18:39

May the words of my mouth and the meditation of my heart be pleasing in your sight, O LORD, my Rock and my Redeemer.

Psalm 19:14

The LORD gives strength to his people; the LORD blesses his people with peace.

Psalm 29:11

Sing for joy to God our strength; shout aloud to the God of Jacob!

Psalm 81:1

My flesh and my heart may fail, but God is the strength of my heart and my portion forever.

Psalm 73:26

A wise man has great power, and a man of knowledge increases strength.

Proverbs 24:5

Do not answer a fool according to his folly, or you will be like him yourself.

Proverbs 26:4

He gives strength to the weary and increases the power of the weak.

Isaiah 40:29

But he said to me, "My grace is sufficient for you, for my power is made perfect in weakness." Therefore I will boast all the more gladly about my weaknesses, so that Christ's power may rest on me.

2 Corinthians 12:9

Summon your power, O God; show us your strength, O God, as you have done before.

Psalm 68:28

Finally, be strong in the Lord and in his mighty power.

Ephesians 6:10

Finding Wisdom When You Need It

I keep asking that the God of our LORD Jesus Christ, the glorious Father, may give you the Spirit of wisdom and revelation, so that you may know him better.

I pray also that the eyes of your heart may be enlightened in order that you may know the hope to which he has called you, the riches of his glorious inheritance in the saints,

And his incomparably great power for us who believe. That power is like the working of his mighty strength.

Ephesians 1:17-19

For this reason, since the day we heard about you, we have not stopped praying for you and asking God to fill you with the knowledge of his will through all spiritual wisdom and understanding.

Colossians 1:9

If any of you lacks wisdom, he should ask God, who gives generously to all without finding fault, and it will be given to him.

But when he asks, he must believe and not doubt, because he who doubts is like a wave of the sea, blown and tossed by the wind.

That man should not think he will receive anything from the LORD;

He is a double-minded man, unstable in all he does.

James 1:5-8

Such "wisdom" does not come down from heaven but is earthly, unspiritual, of the devil.

For where you have envy and selfish ambition, there you find disorder and every evil practice.

But the wisdom that comes from heaven is first of all pure; then peace-loving, considerate, submissive, full of mercy and good fruit, impartial and sincere.

Peacemakers who sow in peace raise a harvest of righteousness.

James 3:15-18

Whoever loves his brother lives in the light, and there is nothing in him to make him stumble.

But whoever hates his brother is in the darkness and walks around in the darkness; he does not know where he is going, because the darkness has blinded him.

1 John 2:10,11

Call to me and I will answer you and tell you great and unsearchable things you do not know.

Jeremiah 33:3

But you have an anointing from the Holy One, and all of you know the truth.

1 John 2:20

As for you, the anointing you received from him remains in you, and you do not need anyone to teach you. But as his anointing teaches you about all things and as that anointing is real, not counterfeit — just as it has taught you, remain in him.

1 John 2:27

Whether you turn to the right or to the left, your ears will hear a voice behind you, saying, "This is the way; walk in it."

Isaiah 30:21

Do not bring hastily to court, for what will you do in the end if your neighbor puts you to shame?

If you argue your case with a neighbor, do not betray another man's confidence.

Proverbs 25:8,9

Like an earring of gold or an ornament of fine gold is a wise man's rebuke to a listening ear.

Proverbs 25:12

I will instruct you and teach you in the way you should go; I will counsel you and watch over you.

Psalm 32:8

For with you is the fountain of life; in your light we see light.

Psalm 36:9

The unfolding of your words gives light; it gives understanding to the simple.

Psalm 119:130

If you had responded to my rebuke, I would have poured out my heart to you and made my thoughts known to you.

Proverbs 1:23

For the LORD gives wisdom, and from his mouth come knowledge and understanding.

He holds victory in store for the upright, he is a shield to those whose walk is blameless.

Proverbs 2:6,7

Send forth your light and your truth, let them guide me; let them bring me to your holy mountain, to the place where you dwell.

Psalm 43:3

Reflect on what I am saying, for the Lord will give you insight into all this.

2 Timothy 2:7

Finding the Presence of God When You Do Not Feel It

The LORD replied, "My Presence will go with you, and I will give you rest."

Exodus 33:14

And teaching them to obey everything I have commanded you. And surely I am with you always, to the very end of the age.

Matthew 28:20

Keep your lives free from the love of money and be content with what you have, because God has said, "Never will I leave you; never will I forsake you."

Hebrews 13:5

A man of many companions may come to ruin, but there is a friend who sticks closer than a brother.

Proverbs 18:24

Greater love has no one than this, that he lay down his life for his friends.

You are my friends if you do what I command.

I no longer call you servants, because a servant does not know his master's business. Instead, I have called you friends, for everything that I learned from my Father I have made known to you.

John 15:13,14

Have I not commanded you? Be strong and courageous. Do not be terrified; do not be discouraged, the LORD your God will be with you wherever you go.

Joshua 1:9

The LORD is near to all who call on him, to all who call on him in truth.

Psalm 145:18

And without faith it is impossible to please God, because anyone who comes to him must believe that he exists and that he rewards those who earnestly seek him.

Hebrews 11:6

All that the Father gives me will come to me, and whoever comes to me I will never drive away.

John 6:37

Come near to God and he will come near to you. Wash your hands, you sinners, and purify your hearts, you double-minded.

James 4:8

Here I am! I stand at the door and knock. If anyone hears my voice and opens the door, I will come in and eat with him, and he with me.

Revelation 3:20

You will seek me and find me when you seek me with all your heart.

Jeremiah 29:13

The LORD is good to those whose hope is in him, to the one who seeks him.

Lamentations 3:25

Promises That God Will Always Hear You

Moreover, I have heard the groaning of the Israelites, whom the Egyptians are enslaving, and I have remembered my covenant.

Exodus 6:5

If my people, who are called by my name, will humble themselves and pray and seek my face and turn from their wicked ways, then will I hear from heaven and will forgive their sin and will heal their land.

2 Chronicles 7:14

You will pray to him, and he will hear you, and you will fulfill your vows.

Job 22:27

Those who know you name will trust in you, for you, LORD have never forsaken those who seek you.

Psalm 9:10

You hear, O LORD, the desire of the afflicted; you encourage them, and you listen to their cry.

Psalm 10:17

The eyes of the LORD are on the righteous and his ears are attentive to their cry;

The righteous cry out, and the LORD hears them; he delivers them from all their troubles.

Psalm 34:15,17

Evening, morning and noon I cry out in distress, and he hears my voice.

Psalm 55:17

O you who hear prayer, to all men will come.

Psalm 65:2

Again, I tell you that if two of you on earth agree about anything you ask for, it will be done for you by my Father in heaven.

For where two or three come together in my name, there am I with them.

Matthew 18:19,20

The LORD hears the needy and does not despise his captive people.

Psalm 69:33

Hear my prayer, O LORD; listen to my cry for mercy.

Psalm 86:6

He will respond to the prayer of the destitute; he will not despise their plea.

Psalm 102:17

The LORD is near to all who call on him, to all who call on him in truth.

He fulfills the desires of those who fear him; he hears their cry and saves them.

Psalm 145:18,19

Before they call I will answer; while they are still speaking I will hear.

Isaiah 65:24

Call to me and I will answer you and tell you great and unsearchable things you do not know.

Jeremiah 33:3

This third I will bring into the fire; I will refine them like silver and test them like gold. They will call on my name and I will answer them; I will say, "They are my people." and they will say, "the LORD is our God."

Zechariah 13:9

But when you pray, go into your room, close the door and pray to your Father, who is unseen. Then your Father, who sees what is done in secret, will reward you.

Do not be like them, for your Father knows what you need before you ask him.

Matthew 6:6,8

Promises for Protection

He who dwells in the shelter of the Most High will rest in the shadow of the Almighty.

I will say of the LORD, "He is my refuge and my fortress, my God, in whom I trust."

Surely he will save you from the fowler's snare and from the deadly pestilence.

He will cover you with his feathers, and under his wings you will find refuge; his faithfulness will be your shield and rampart.

You will not fear the terror of night, nor the arrow that flies by day,

Nor the pestilence that stalks in the darkness, nor the plague that destroys at midday.

A thousand may fall at your side, ten thousand at your right hand, but it will not come near you.

You will only observe with your eyes and see the punishment of the wicked.

If you make the Most High your dwelling — even the LORD, who is my refuge —

Then no harm will befall you, no disaster will come near your tent.

For he will command his angels concerning you to guard you in all your ways;

They will lift you up in their hands, so that you will not strike your foot against a stone.

You will tread upon the lion and the cobra; you will trample the great lion and the serpent.

"Because he loves me," says the LORD, "I will rescue him; I will protect him, for he acknowledges my name.

He will call upon me, and I will answer him; I will be with him in trouble, I will deliver him and honor him.

With long life will I satisfy him and show him my salvation."

Psalm 91:1-16

Therefore let everyone who is godly pray to you while you may be found; surely when the mighty waters rise, they will not reach him.

You are my hiding place; you will protect me from trouble and surround me with songs of deliverance. *Selah*

Psalm 32:6,7

God is our refuge and strength, an ever-present help in trouble.

Therefore we will not fear, though the earth give way and the mountains fall into the heart of the sea.

Psalm 46:1,2

As for God, his way is perfect; the word of the LORD is flawless. He is a shield for all who take refuge in him.

2 Samuel 22:31

That is why I am suffering as I am. Yet I am not ashamed, because I know whom I have believed, and am convinced that he is able to guard what I have entrusted to him for that day.

2 Timothy 1:12

To him who is able to keep you from falling and to present you before his glorious presence without fault and with great joy.

Jude 24

Promises for When You Need Healing

Surely he took up our infirmities and carried our sorrows, yet we considered him stricken by God, smitten by him, and afflicted.

But he was pierced for our transgressions, he was crushed for our iniquities; the punishment that brought us peace was upon him, and by his wounds we are healed.

Isaiah 53:4,5

When evening came, many who were demon-possessed were brought to him, and he drove out the spirits with a word and healed all the sick.

This was to fulfill what was spoken through the prophet Isaiah: "He took up our infirmities and carried our diseases."

Matthew 8:16,17

He himself bore our sins in his body on the tree, so that we might die to sins and live for righteousness; by his wounds you have been healed.

1 Peter 2:24

Christ redeemed us from the curse of the law by becoming a curse for us, for it is written: "Cursed is everyone who is hung on a tree."

Galatians 3:13

He said, "If you listen carefully to the voice of the LORD your God and do what is right in his eyes, if you pay attention to his commands and keep all his decrees, I will not bring on you any of the diseases I brought on the Egyptians, for I am the LORD, who heals you."

Exodus 15:26

Worship the LORD your God, and his blessing will be on your food and water. I will take away sickness from among you,

And none will miscarry or be barren in your land. I will give you a full life span.

Exodus 23:25,26

Then no harm will befall you, no disaster will come near your tent.

Psalm 91:10

With long life will I satisfy him and show him my salvation.
Psalm 91:16

Praise the LORD, O my soul, and forget not all his benefits —

Who forgives all your sins and heals all your diseases.
Psalm 103:2-3

He sent forth his word and healed them; he rescued them from the grave.
Psalm 107:20

So is my word that goes out from my mouth: It will not return to me empty, but will accomplish what I desire and achieve the purpose for which I sent it.
Isaiah 55:11

Every good and perfect gift is from above, coming down from the Father of the heavenly lights, who does not change like shifting shadows.
James 1:17

A man with leprosy came and knelt before him and said ,"LORD, if you are willing, you can make me clean."

Jesus reached out his hand and touched the man. "I am willing," he said. "Be clean!" Immediately he was cured of his leprosy.
Matthew 8:2,3

How God anointed Jesus of Nazareth with the Holy Spirit and power, and how he went around doing good and healing all who were under the power of the devil, because God was with him.

Acts 10:38

The thief comes only to steal and kill and destroy; I have come that they may have life, and have it to the full.

John 10:10

Jesus heard that they had thrown him out, and when he found him, he said, "Do you believe in the Son of Man?"

John 9:35

Jesus Christ is the same yesterday and today and forever.

Hebrews 13:8

I tell you the truth, anyone who has faith in me will do what I have been doing. He will do even greater things than these, because I am going to the Father.

John 14:12

Is any one of you sick? He should call the elders of the church to pray over him and anoint him with oil in the name of the Lord.

And the prayer offered in faith will make the sick person well; the Lord will raise him up. If he has sinned, he will be forgiven.

James 5:14,15

Promises for Deliverance

My soul finds rest in God alone; my salvation comes from him.

He alone is my rock and my salvation; he is my fortress, I will never be shaken.

Psalm 62:1,2

Find rest, O my soul, in God alone; my hope comes from him.

He alone is my rock and my salvation; he is my fortress, I will not be shaken.

My salvation and my honor depend on God; he is my mighty rock, my refuge.

Trust in him at all times, O people; pour out your hearts to him, for God is our refuge. *Selah*

Psalm 62:5-8

One thing God has spoken, two things have I heard: that you, O God, are strong,

And that you, O LORD, are loving. Surely you will reward each person according to what he has done.

Psalm 62:11,12

If this is so, then the Lord knows how to rescue godly men from trials and to hold the unrighteous for the day of judgement, while continuing their punishment.

2 Peter 2:9

He reached down from on high and took hold of me; he drew me out of deep waters.

He rescued me from my powerful enemy, from my foes, who were too strong for me.

They confronted me in the day of my disaster, but the LORD was my support.

He brought me out into a spacious place; he rescued me because he delighted in me.

Psalm 18:16-18

In the shelter of your presence you hide them from the intrigues of men; in your dwelling you keep them safe from accusing tongues.

Psalm 31:20

I sought the LORD, and he answered me; he delivered me from all my fears.

Psalm 34:4

A righteous man may have many troubles, but the LORD delivers him from them all.

Psalm 34:19

To the Jews who had believed him, Jesus said, "If you hold to my teaching, you are really my disciples.

"Then you will know the truth, and the truth will set you free."

John 8:31,32

When Jesus had called the Twelve together, he gave them power and authority to drive out all demons and to cure diseases.

Luke 9:1

He called his twelve disciples to him and gave them authority to drive out evil spirits and to heal every disease and sickness.

Matthew 10:1

I have given you authority to trample on snakes and scorpions and to overcome all the power of the enemy; nothing will harm you.

Luke 10:19

When evening came, many who were demon-possessed were brought to him, and he drove out the spirits with a word and healed all the sick.

This was to fulfill what was spoken through the prophet Isaiah: "He took up our infirmities and carried our diseases."

Matthew 8:16,17

The Lord will rescue me from every evil attack and will bring me safely to his heavenly kingdom. To him be glory for ever and ever. Amen.

2 Timothy 4:18

Overcoming Past Bad Memories

Do not conform any longer to the pattern of this world, but be transformed by the renewing of your mind. Then you will be able to test and approve what God's will is — his good, pleasing and perfect will.

Romans 12:2

Therefore, if anyone is in Christ, he is a new creation; the old has gone, the new has come!

2 Corinthians 5:17

Brothers, I do not consider myself yet to have taken hold of it. But one thing I do: Forgetting what is behind and straining toward what is ahead.

Philippians 3:13

See, I am doing a new thing! Now it springs up; do you not perceive it? I am making a way in the desert and streams in the wasteland.

Isaiah 43:19

See, for former things have taken place, and new things I declare; before they spring into being I announce them to you.

Isaiah 42:9

See! The winter is past; the rains are over and gone.

Song of Songs 2:11

God presented him as a sacrifice of atonement, through faith in his blood. He did this to demonstrate his justice, because in his forbearance he had left the sins committed beforehand unpunished .

Romans 3:25

To be made new in the attitude of your minds.

Ephesians 4:23

Being Close To God

The LORD is good to those whose hope is in him, to the one who seeks him.

Lamentations 3:25

You will seek me and find me when you seek me with all your heart.

Jeremiah 29:13

Come near to God and he will come near to you. Wash your hand, you sinners, and purify your hearts, you double-minded.

James 4:8

But if from there you seek the LORD your God, you will find him if you look for him with all your heart and with all your soul.

Deuteronomy 4:29

He sought God during the days of Zechariah, who instructed him in the fear of

God. As long as he sought the LORD, God gave him success.

2 Chronicles 26:5

One thing I ask of the LORD this is what I seek; that I may dwell in the house of the LORD all the days of my life, to gaze upon the beauty of the LORD and to seek him in his temple.

For in the day of trouble he will keep me safe in his dwelling; he will hide me in the shelter of his tabernacle and set me high upon a rock.

Then my head will be exalted above the enemies who surround me; at his tabernacle will I sacrifice with shouts of joy; I will sing and make music to the LORD.

Hear my voice when I call, O LORD; be merciful to me and answer me.

My heart says of you, "Seek his face!" Your face, LORD, I will seek.

Psalm 27:4-8

As the deer pants for streams of water, so my soul pants for you, O God.

My soul thirsts for God, for the living God. when can I go and meet with God?

Psalm 42:1,2

O God, you are my God, earnestly I seek you; my soul thirsts for you, my body longs for you, in a dry and weary land where there is no water.

I have seen you in the sanctuary and beheld your power and your glory.

Psalm 63:1,2

The LORD is near to all who call on him, to all who call on him in truth.

Psalm 145:18

It was not by their sword that they won the land, nor did their arm bring them victory; it was your right hand, your arm, and the light of your face, for you loved them.

Psalm 44:3

Blessed are those who hunger and thirst for righteousness, for they will be filled.

Matthew 5:6

God did this so that men would seek him and perhaps reach out for him and find him, though he is not far from each one of us.

Acts 17:27

The Spirit and the bride say, "Come!" And let him who hears say, "Come!"

Whoever is thirsty, let him come; and whoever wishes, let him take the free gift of the water of life.

Revelation 22:17

PART VI

31-DAY DEVOTIONAL

By
John Mason

DAY 1

YOUR LEAST FAVORITE COLOR
SHOULD BE BEIGE

Never try to defend your present position and situation. Choose to be a person who is on the offensive, not the defensive. **People who live defensively never rise above being average.** We're called, as Christians, to be on the offensive, to take the initiative. A lukewarm, indecisive person is never secure regardless of his wealth, education, or position.

Don't ever let your quest for balance become an excuse for not taking the unique, radical, invading move that God has directed you to take. Many times the attempt to maintain balance in life is really just an excuse for being lukewarm. In Joshua 1:6,7,9 the Lord says three times to Joshua, "Be strong and courageous." I believe that He is saying the same thing to all believers today.

When you choose to be on the offensive, the atmosphere of your life will begin to change. So if you don't like the atmosphere of your life, choose to take the offensive position. Taking the offensive is not just an action taken outside a person; it is always a decision made within.

When you do choose to be on the offensive, keep all your conflicts impersonal. Fight the issue, not the person. Speak about what God in you can do, not what others cannot do. **You will find that when all of your reasons are defensive, your cause almost never succeeds.**

Being on the offensive and taking the initiative is a master key which opens the door to opportunity in your life. Learn to create a habit of taking the initiative and **don't ever start your day in neutral**. Every morning when your feet hit the floor, you should be thinking on the offensive, reacting like an invader, taking control of your day and your life.

By pulling back and being defensive usually you enhance the problem. Intimidation always precedes defeat. If you are not sure which way to go, pray and move towards the situation in confident trust.

Be like the two fishermen who got trapped in a storm in the middle of the lake. One turned to the other and asked, "Should we pray, or should we row?" His wise companion responded, "Let's do both!"

That's taking the offensive.

DAY 2

GROWTH COMES FROM BUILDING ON TALENTS, GIFTS, AND STRENGTHS — NOT BY SOLVING PROBLEMS

One of the most neglected areas in many people's lives is the area of gifts that God has placed within them. It is amazing how some people can devote their entire lives to a field of endeavor or a profession that has nothing to do with their inborn talents. In fact, the opposite is also true. Many people spend their whole lifetime trying to change who God has made them. They ignore their God-given talents while continually seeking to change their natural makeup. As children of God, we need to recognize our innate gifts, talents, and strengths and do everything in our power to build on them.

One good thing about God's gifts and calling is that they are permanent and enduring. Romans 11:29 tells us: *...the gifts and calling of God are without repentance.* The Greek word translated *repentance* in this verse means "irrevocable." God cannot take away His gifts and calling in your life. **Even if you've never done anything with them, even if you've failed time and time again, God's gifts and calling are still resident within you.** They are there this day, and you can choose to do something with them, beginning right now.

Gifts and talents are really God's deposits in our personal accounts, but we determine the interest on them. The greater the amount of interest and attention we give to them, the greater their value becomes. **God's gifts are never loans; they are always deposits.** As such, they are never used up or depleted. In fact, the more they are used, the greater, stronger, and more valuable they become. When they are put to good use, they provide information, insight, and revelation which cannot be received any other way or from any other source.

As Christians, we need to make full use of all the gifts and talents which God has bestowed upon us so that we do not abound in one area while becoming bankrupt in another. Someone has said, "If the only tool you have is a hammer, you tend to treat everything like a nail." Don't make that mistake; use all of the gifts God has given you. If you choose not to step out and make maximum use of the gifts and talents in your life, you will spend your days on this earth helping someone else reach his goals. Most people let others control their destiny. Don't allow anyone to take over the driver's seat in your life. Fulfill your own dreams and determine your own life's course.

Never underestimate the power of the gifts that are within you. **Gifts and talents are given us to use not only so we can fulfill to the fullest the call in our own lives, but also so we can reach the souls who are attached to those gifts.** There are people whose lives are waiting to be affected by what God has placed within you. So evaluate yourself. Define and refine your gifts, talents and strengths. Choose today to look for opportunities to exercise your unique God-endowed, God-ordained gifts and calling.

DAY 3

"THE NOSE OF THE BULLDOG IS SLANTED BACKWARDS SO HE CAN CONTINUE TO BREATHE WITHOUT LETTING GO" — WINSTON CHURCHILL

Persistent people begin their success where most others quit. We Christians need to be known as people of persistence and endurance. **One person with commitment, persistence, and endurance will accomplish more than a thousand people with interest alone.** In Hebrews 12:1 (NIV) we read: *Therefore, since we are surrounded by such a great cloud of witnesses, let us throw off everything that hinders and the sin that so easily entangles, and let us run with perseverance the race marked out for us.* The more diligently we work, the harder it is to quit. Persistence is a habit; so is quitting.

Never worry about how much money, ability, or equipment you are starting with. Just begin with a million dollars worth of determination. Remember: **it's not what you have, it's what you do with what you have that makes all the difference.** Many people eagerly begin "the good fight of faith," but they forget to add patience, persistence, and endurance to their enthusiasm. Josh Billings said, "Consider the postage stamp. Its usefulness consists in the ability to stick to something until it gets there." You and I should be known as "postage-stamp" Christians.

In First Corinthians 15:58, the Apostle Paul writes: *Therefore, my beloved brethren, be ye stedfast, unmoveable, always abounding in the work of the Lord, forasmuch as ye know that your labour is not in vain in the Lord.* Peter tells us: *Wherefore, beloved, seeing that ye look for such things, be diligent that ye may be found of him in peace, without spot, and blameless* (2 Pet. 3:14). And wise Solomon points out: *Seest thou a man diligent in his business? he shall stand before kings...*(Prov. 22:29).

In the Far East the people plant a tree called the Chinese bamboo. During the first four years they water and fertilize the plant with seemingly little or no results. Then the fifth year they again apply water and fertilizer — and in five weeks' time the tree grows ninety feet in height! The obvious question is: did the Chinese bamboo tree grow ninety feet in five weeks, or did it grow ninety feet in five years? The answer is: it grew ninety feet in five years. Because if at any time during those five years the people had stopped watering and fertilizing the tree, it would have died.

Many times our dreams and plans appear not to be succeeding. We are tempted to give up and quit trying. Instead, we need to continue to water and fertilize those dreams and plans, nurturing the seeds of the vision God has placed within us. Because we know that if we do not quit, if we display perseverance and endurance, we will also reap a harvest. Charles Haddon Spurgeon said, "By perseverance the snail reached the ark." We need to be like that snail.

DAY 4

WE CAN GROW BY OUR QUESTIONS, AS WELL AS BY OUR ANSWERS

Here are some important questions we should ask ourselves:

1. What one decision would I make if I knew that it would not fail?

2. What one thing should I eliminate from my life because it holds me back from reaching my full potential?

3. Am I on the path of something absolutely marvelous, or something absolutely mediocre?

4. If everyone in the United States of America were on my level of spirituality, would there be a revival in the land?

5. Does the devil know who I am?

6. Am I running from something, or to something?

7. What can I do to make better use of my time?

8. Would I recognize Jesus if I met Him on the street?

9. Who do I need to forgive?

10. What is my favorite scripture for myself, my family, my career?

11. What impossible thing am I believing and planning for?

12. What is my most prevailing thought?

13. What good thing have I previously committed myself to do that I have quit doing?

14. Of the people I respect most, what is it about them that earns my respect?

15. What would a truly creative person do in my situation?

16. What outside influences are causing me to be better or worse?

17. Can I lead anyone else to Christ?

18. In what areas do I need improvement in terms of personal development?

19. What gifts, talents, or strengths do I have?

20. What is one thing that I can do for someone else who has no opportunity to repay me?

DAY 5

DON'T ASK TIME WHERE IT'S GON. TELL IT WHERE TO GO

All great achievers, all successful people, are those who have been able to gain control over their time. It has been said that all human beings have been created equal in one respect: each person has been given 24 hours each day.

We need to choose to give our best time to our most challenging situation. It's not how much we do that matters; it's how much we get done. We should choose to watch our time, not our watch. One of the best timesavers is the ability to say no. Not saying no when you should is one of the biggest wastes of time you will ever experience.

Don't spend a dollar's worth of time for ten cents' worth of results.

Make sure to take care of the vulnerable times in your days. These vulnerable times are the first thing in the morning and the last thing at night. I have heard a minister say that what a person is like at midnight when he is all alone reveals that person's true self.

Never allow yourself to say, "I could be doing big things if I weren't so busy doing small things!" Take control of your time. **The greater control you exercise over your time, the greater freedom you will experience in your life.** The psalmist prayed, *So teach us to number our days, that we may apply our hearts unto wisdom* (Ps. 90:12). The Bible teaches us that the devil comes to steal, and to kill, and to destroy (John 10:10), and this verse applies to time as well as to people. The enemy desires to provide God's children with ideas of how to kill, steal, and destroy valuable time.

People are always saying, "I'd give anything to be able to. . ." There is a basic leadership principle that says, "6 x 1 = 6." If you want to write a book, learn to play a musical instrument, become a better tennis player, or do anything else important, then you should devote one hour a day, six days a week, to the project. Sooner than you think, what you desire will become reality. There are not many things that a person cannot accomplish in 312 hours a year! Just a commitment of one hour a day, six days a week, is all it takes.

We all have the same amount of time each day. The difference between people is determined by what they do with the amount of time at their disposal. Don't be like the airline pilot flying over the Pacific Ocean who reported to his passengers, "We're lost, but we're making great time!" Remember that the future arrives an hour at a time. **Gain control of your time, and you will gain control of your life.**

DAY 6

DON'T CONSUME YOUR TOMORROWS FEEDING ON YOUR YESTERDAYS

Decide today to get rid of any "loser's limps" which you may still be carrying from some past experience. As followers of Jesus Christ, you and I need to break the power of the past to dominate our present and determine our future.

In Luke 9:62, Jesus said, *...No man, having put his hand to the plough, and looking back, is fit for the kingdom of God.* If we are not careful, we will allow the past to exercise a great hold on us. **The more we look backward, the less able we are to see forward.** The past makes no difference concerning what God can do for us today.

That is the beauty of the Christian life. Even when we have failed, we are able to ask for forgiveness and be totally cleansed of and released from our past actions. Whatever hold the past may have on us can be broken. It is never God who holds us back. It is always our own choosing to allow the past to keep us from living to the fullest in the present and future. Failure is waiting around the corner for those who are living off of yesterday's successes and failures. **We should choose to be forward-focused, not past-possessed**. We should learn to profit from the past, but to invest in the future.

In Philippians 3:13,14, the Apostle Paul writes:

Brethren, I count not myself to have apprehended: but this one thing I do, forgetting those things which are behind, and reaching forth unto those things which are before,

I press toward the mark for the prize of the high calling of God in Christ Jesus.

The key here is "forgetting those things which are behind" in order to reach for "the high calling of God in Christ Jesus." To fulfill our calling in Christ, we must first forget that which lies behind. Probably the most common stronghold in a person's life is his past mistakes and failures. Today is the day to begin to shake off the shackles of the past and move forward.

The past is past. It has no life.

DAY 7

THE BEST TIME OF DAY IS NOW

Procrastination is a killer.

When you choose to kill time, you begin to kill those gifts and callings which God has placed within your life. *The Living Bible* paraphrase of Ecclesiastes 11:4 reads: *If you wait for perfect conditions, you will never get anything done.*

The first step in overcoming procrastination is to eliminate all excuses and reasons for not taking decisive and immediate action.

Everybody is on the move. They are moving forwards, backwards, or on a treadmill. The mistake most people make is thinking that the main goal of life is to stay busy. Such thinking is a trap. What is important is not whether a person is busy, but whether he is progressing. It is a question of activity versus accomplishment.

A gentleman named John Henry Fabre conducted an experiment with processionary caterpillars. They are so named because of their peculiar habit of blindly following each other no matter how they are lined up or where they are going. This man took a group of these tiny creatures and did something interesting with them. He placed them in a circle. For 24 hours the caterpillars dutifully followed one another around and around. Then he did something else. He placed the caterpillars around a saucer full of pine needles (their favorite food). For six days the mindless creatures moved around and around the saucer, literally dying from starvation and exhaustion even though an abundance of choice food was located less than two inches away.

You see, they had confused activity with accomplishment.

We Christians need to be known as those who accomplish great things for God — not those who simply talk about it. Procrastinators are good at talking versus doing. It is true what Mark Twain said: "Noise produces nothing. Often a hen who has merely laid an egg cackles as though she has laid an asteroid."

We need to be like the apostles. They were never known much for their policies or procedures, their theories or excuses. Instead, they were known for their acts. Many people say that they are waiting for God; but in most cases God is waiting for them. We need to say with the psalmist, "Lord, my times are in Your hands." (Ps. 31:15.) The price of growth is always less than the cost of stagnation. As Edmund Burke said, "The only thing necessary for the triumph of evil is for good men to do nothing."

Occasionally you may see someone who doesn't do anything, and yet seems to be successful in life. Don't be deceived. The old saying is true: "Even a broken clock is right twice a day." As Christians we are called to make progress — not excuses.

Procrastination is a primary tool of the devil to hold us back and to make us miss God's timing in our lives. *The desire of the slothful killeth him; for his hands refuse to labour* (Prov. 21:25). **The fact is, the longer we take to act on God's direction, the more unclear it becomes.**

DAY 8

FEAR AND WORRY ARE INTEREST PAID IN ADVANCE ON SOMETHING YOU MAY NEVER OWN

Fear is a poor chisel to carve out tomorrow. Worry is simply the triumph of fear over faith.

There's a story that is told about a woman who was standing on a street corner crying profusely. A man came up to her and asked why she was weeping. The lady shook her head and replied: "I was just thinking that maybe someday I would get married. We would later have a beautiful baby girl. Then one day this child and I would go for a walk along this street, come to this corner, and my darling daughter would run into the street, get hit by a car, and die."

Now that sounds like a pretty ridiculous situation — for a grown woman to be weeping her eyes out because of something that would probably never happen. Yet isn't this the way we respond when we worry? We take a situation or event which might never exist and build it up all out of proportion in our mind.

There is an old Swedish proverb that says, "Worry gives a small thing a big shadow." **Worry is simply the misuse of God's creative imagination which He has placed within each of us.** When fear rises in our mind, we should learn to expect the opposite in our life.

The word *worry* itself is derived from an Anglo-Saxon term meaning "to strangle," or "to choke off." There is no question that worry and fear in the mind does choke off the creative flow from above.

Things are seldom as they seem. "Skim milk masquerades as cream," said W.S. Gilbert. As we dwell on and worry about matters beyond our control, a negative effect begins to set in. Too much analysis always leads to paralysis. *Worry is a route which leads from somewhere to nowhere. Don't let it direct your life.*

In Psalm 55:22 the Bible says, *Cast thy burden upon the Lord, and he shall sustain thee: he shall never suffer the righteous to be moved.* Never respond out of fear, and never fear to respond. Action attacks fear; inaction builds fear.

Don't worry and don't fear. Instead, take your fear and worry to the Lord, *Casting all your care upon him; for he careth for you* (1 Pet. 5:7).

DAY 9

OUR WORDS ARE SEED PLANTED INTO OTHER PEOPLE'S LIVES

What we say is important. The Bible states that out of the abundance of the heart the mouth speaks. (Matt. 12:34.) We need to change our vocabulary. We need to speak words of life and light. Our talk should always rise to the level of the Word of God.

We Christians should be known as people who speak positively, those who speak the Word of God into situations, those who speak forth words of life.

We should not be like the man who joined a monastery in which the monks were allowed to speak only two words every seven years. After the first seven years had passed, the new initiate met with the abbot who asked him, "Well, what are your two words?"

"Food's bad," replied the man, who then went back to spend another seven-year period before once again meeting with his ecclesiastical superior.

"What are your two words now?" asked the clergyman.

"Bed's hard," responded the man.

Seven years later — twenty-one years after his initial entry into the monastery — the man met with the abbot for the third and final time.

"And what are your two words this time?" he was asked.

"I quit."

"Well, I'm not surprised," answered the disgusted cleric, "all you've done since you got here is complain!"

Don't be like that man; don't be known as a person whose only words are negative.

If you are a member of the "murmuring grapevine," you need to resign. In John 6:43 our Lord instructed His disciples, ...*Murmur not among yourselves*. In Philippians 2:14,15 the Apostle Paul exhorted the believers of his day:

Do all things without murmurings and disputings:

That ye may be blameless and harmless, the sons of God, without rebuke, in the midst of a crooked and perverse nation, among whom ye shine as lights in the world.

Contrary to what you may have heard, talk is not cheap. Talk is very expensive. We should know that our words are powerful. What we say affects what we get from others, and what others get from us. When we speak the wrong word, it lessens our ability to see and hear the will of God.

DAY 10

VERSUS

Every day we make decisions. Daily we are confronted with options. **We must choose one or the other.** We cannot have both. These options include:

Being bitter versus being better.

Indifference versus decisiveness.

Lukewarmness versus enthusiasm.

"If we can" versus "how we can."

"Give up" versus "get up."

Security versus risk.

Coping with evil versus overcoming evil.

Blending in versus standing out.

How much we do versus how much we get done.

Coexisting with darkness versus opposing darkness.

Destruction versus development.

Resisting versus receiving.

Complaining versus obtaining.

Trying versus committing.

Peace versus strife.

Choice versus chance.

Determination versus discouragement.

Growing versus dying.

Demanding more of ourselves versus excusing ourselves.

Doing for others versus doing for self.

Progress versus regression.

Steering versus drifting.

Priorities versus aimlessness.

Accountability versus irresponsibility.

Action versus activity.

Solutions versus problems.

More of God versus more of everything else.

Being in "Who's Who" versus asking "Why me?"

DAY 11

KEEP YOUR FEET ON THE ROCK
WHEN YOU REACH THE END
OF YOUR ROPE

Don't quit. There is a big difference between quitting and changing. I believe that **when God sees someone who doesn't quit, He looks down and says, "There is someone I can use."**

In Galatians 6:9 (NIV) we are told, *Let us not become weary in doing good, for at the proper time we will reap a harvest if we do not give up.* Look at this verse carefully. It urges us not to become weary, assuring us that we will — not might — reap a harvest if we do not give up.

God doesn't quit. It is impossible for Him to do so. In Philippians 1:6 (NIV) the Apostle Paul writes about *being confident of this, that he who began a good work in you will carry it on to completion until the day of Christ Jesus.* There are several important points in this verse. The most crucial is the fact that God does not quit. Therefore, we can have great confidence that He will complete the good work He has begun in us. He will see us through every step of the way until we have reached our ultimate destination.

One of the best scriptural examples of a person who did not quit is Joseph. He had many reasons to justify giving up. First, when he was trapped in the pit into which his brothers had thrown him because of their jealousy, I am sure he said to himself, "This is not the way I dreamed my life would work out." Later on, he had a marvelous opportunity to become discouraged and quit when he was unjustly accused and thrown into prison for a crime he did not commit. Again he could have said to himself, "This is not right; I'm not supposed to be here."

But eventually the dream which God had given Joseph became reality. He was elevated from prisoner to prime minister in one day. Although Joseph did not know or understand the steps through which the Lord would lead him, he remained true to his God. Despite the trials and obstacles he faced, he did not quit.

There is no greater reward than that which comes as a result of holding fast to the Word and will of God. Only you can decide not to lose. Most people quit right on the verge of success. Often it is right at their fingertips. There is only one degree of difference between hot water and steam.

In Luke 18 (NIV) Jesus told the parable of the persistent widow. The Bible reveals His purpose in relating this story: *Then Jesus told his disciples a parable to show them they should always pray and not give up* (v. 1). The psalmist tells us, *Commit thy way unto the Lord; trust also in him; and he shall bring it to pass* (Ps. 37:5).

The only way we can lose is to quit. That is the only decision we can make that can keep us from reaching God's goals in our lives.

DAY 12

A GOAL IS A DREAM
WITH A DEADLINE

In Habakkuk 2:2 the Lord tells the prophet, ...*Write the vision, and make it plain upon tables, that he may run that readeth it*. The key to successful goal-setting is revealed in this scripture.

First, the vision must be written down. When you keep a vision in your mind, it is not really a goal; it is really nothing more than a dream. There is power in putting that dream down on paper. When you commit something to writing, commitment to achievement naturally follows. You can't start a fire with paper alone, but writing something down on paper can start a fire inside of you.

God Himself followed His Word here, by taking His vision for us and having it put down on paper in the form of the Bible. He did not just rely on the Holy Spirit to guide and direct us; He put His goals down in writing. We are told to make the word of the Lord plain upon "tables" (tablets) so that it is clear and specific as to what the vision is "...so that he may run that readeth it."

The key word is "run." God desires that we run with the vision and goal in our life. As long as we are running with the vision, we won't turn around. When you walk with a vision, it's easy to change directions and go the wrong way. **You can't stroll to a goal.**

In Proverbs 24:3,4 (TLB), we read: *Any enterprise is built by wise planning, becomes strong through common sense, and profits wonderfully by keeping abreast of the facts.* Simply stated, effective goal-setting and planning provides an opportunity to bring the future to the present and deal with it today. You will find that achievement is easy when your outer goals become an inner commitment.

Even though we have the Holy Spirit, we still need to prepare; we are just better equipped to do so. God's first choice for us in any situation cannot be disorder and waste of funds or resources. That's why proper planning is so important. Plan to the potential. Believe for God's biggest dream. When you plan, look to the future, not the past. You can't drive forward by looking out the rear window.

Always involve yourself with some- thing that's bigger than you are, because that's where God is. Every great success was, at the beginning, impossible. We all have opportunity for success in our lives. It takes just as much energy and effort for a bad life as it does for a good life; yet most people live meaningless lives simply because they never decided to write their vision down and then follow through on it. Know this, if you can't see the mark, you can't press towards it.

Ponder the path of thy feet, and let all thy ways be established (Prov. 4:26). You will find that what you learn on the path to your goals is actually more valuable than achieving the goal itself. Columbus discovered America while searching for a route to India. Be on the lookout for the "Americas" in your path. Put God's vision for your life on paper, and begin to run with His plan.

DAY 13

SMILE — IT ADDS TO YOUR
FACE VALUE

Christians should be the happiest, most enthusiastic, people on earth. In fact, the word *enthusiasm* comes from a Greek word, *entheous* which means "God within" or "full of God."

Smiling — being happy and enthusiastic — is always a choice and not a result. It is a decision that must be consciously made. Enthusiasm and joy and happiness will improve your personality and people's opinion of you. It will help you keep a proper perspective on life. Helen Keller said, "Keep your face to the sunshine and you cannot see the shadow."

The bigger the challenge you are facing, the more enthusiasm you need. Philippians 2:5 (NIV) says, *Your attitude should be the same as that of Christ Jesus.* I believe Jesus was a man Who had a smile on His face, a spring in His step, and joy on His countenance.

Our attitude always tells others what we expect in return.

A smile is a powerful weapon. It can even break the ice. You'll find that being happy and enthusiastic is like a head cold — it's very, very contagious. A laugh a day will keep negative people away. You will also find that as enthusiasm increases, stress and fear in your life will decrease. The Bible says that the joy of the Lord is our strength. (Neh. 8:10.)

Many people say, "Well, no wonder that person is happy, confident, and positive; if I had his job and assets, I would be too." Such thinking falsely assumes that successful people are positive because they have a good income and lots of possessions. But the reverse is true. Such people probably have a good income and lots of possessions as a result of being positive, confident, and happy.

Enthusiasm always motivates to action. No significant accomplishment has ever been made without enthusiasm. In John 15:10,11 (NIV) we have a promise from the Lord, *"If you obey my commands, you will remain in my love, just as I have obeyed my Father's commands and remain in his love. I have told you this so that my joy may be in you and that your joy may be complete."*

The joy and love of the Lord are yours — so smile!

DAY 14

DON'T QUIT AFTER A VICTORY

There are two times when a person stops: after a defeat and after a victory. Eliminating this kind of procrastination increases momentum.

Robert Schuller has a good saying: "Don't cash in, cast into deeper water." Don't stop after a success, keep the forward momentum going.

One of the great prizes of victory is the opportunity to do more. The trouble is, we've innoculated ourselves with small doses of success which keep us from catching the real thing.

As I was writing this section on momentum, I couldn't get out of my mind a picture of a large boulder at the top of a hill. This boulder represents our lives. If we rock the boulder back and forth and get it moving, its momentum will make it almost unstoppable. The same is true of us.

The Bible promises us God's divine momentum in our lives. In Philippians 1:6

the Apostle Paul writes, *Being confident of this very thing, that he which hath begun a good work in you will perform it until the day of Jesus Christ.* God's momentum always results in growth.

There are five ways to have divine momentum in your life:

1.   Be fruitful. (2 Cor. 9:10.)

2.   Speak the truth. (Eph. 4:15.)

3.   Be spiritually mature. (Heb. 6:1.)

4.   Crave the Word of God. (1 Pet. 2:2.)

5.   Grow in the grace and knowledge of Jesus. (2 Pet. 3:18.)

God's definition of spiritual momentum is found in 2 Peter 1:5 (NIV):

For this very reason, make every effort to add to your faith goodness; and to goodness, knowledge; and to knowledge, self-control; and to self-control, perseverance; and to perseverance, godliness; and to godliness, brotherly kindness; and to brotherly kindness, love. For if you possess these qualities in increasing measure, they will keep you from being ineffective and unproductive in your knowledge of our Lord Jesus Christ.

Let go of whatever makes you stop.

DAY 15

THE MOST NATURAL THING TO DO WHEN YOU GET KNOCKED DOWN IS TO GET UP

How we respond to failure and mistakes is one of the most important decisions we make every day. Failure doesn't mean that nothing has been accomplished. There is always the opportunity to learn something. What is in you will always be bigger than whatever is around you.

We all experience failure and make mistakes. In fact, successful people always have more failure in their lives than average people do. You will find that throughout history all great people, at some point in their lives, have failed. **Only those who do not expect anything are never disappointed. Only those who never try, never fail.** Anyone who is currently achieving anything in life is simultaneously risking failure. It is always better to fail in doing something than to excel in doing nothing. A flawed diamond is more valuable than a perfect brick. People who have no failures also have few victories.

Everybody gets knocked down, it's how fast he gets up that counts. There is a positive correlation between spiritual maturity and how quickly a person responds to his failures and mistakes. The greater the degree of spiritual maturity, the greater the ability to get back up and go on. The less the spiritual maturity, the longer the individual will continue to hang on to past failures. Every person knows someone who, to this day, is still held back by mistakes he made years ago. God never sees any of us as failures; He only sees us as learners.

We have only failed when we do not learn from the experience. The decision is up to us. We can choose to turn a failure into a hitching post, or a guidepost.

Here is the key to being free from the stranglehold of past failures and mistakes: learn the lesson and forget the details. Gain from the experience, but do not roll over and over in your mind the minute details of it. Build on the experience, and get on with your life.

Remember: **the call is higher than the fall.**

DAY 16

THOSE WHO DON'T TAKE CHANCES DON'T MAKE ADVANCES

All great discoveries have been made by people whose faith ran ahead of their minds. Significant achievements have not been obtained by taking small risks on unimportant issues. Don't ever waste time planning, analyzing, and risking on small ideas. It is always wise to spend more time on decisions that are irreversible and less time on those that are reversible.

Learn to stretch, to reach out where God is. Aim high and take risks. The world's approach is to look to next year based on last year. We Christians need to reach to the potential, not reckon to the past. Those who make great strides are those who take chances and plan toward the challenges of life.

Don't become so caught up in small matters that you can't take advantage of important opportunities. Most people spend their entire lives letting down buckets into empty wells. They continue to waste away their days trying to draw them up again.

Choose today to dream big, to strive to reach the full potential of your calling. Choose to major on the important issues of life, not on the unimportant. H. Stern said, "If you're hunting rabbits in tiger country, you must keep your eye peeled for tigers, but when you are hunting tigers you can ignore the rabbits." There are plenty of tigers to go around. Don't be distracted by or seek after the rabbits of life. Set your sights on "big game."

Security and opportunity are total strangers. If an undertaking doesn't include faith, it's not worthy of being called God's direction. I don't believe that God would call any of us to do anything that would not include an element of faith in Him.

There is a famous old saying that goes, "Even a turtle doesn't get ahead unless he sticks his neck out." **Dream big, because you serve a big God.**

DAY 17

YOUR BEST FRIENDS ARE THOSE WHO BRING OUT THE BEST IN YOU

We need to be careful of the kind of insulation we use in our lives. We need to insulate ourselves from negative people and ideas. But, we should never insulate ourselves from godly counsel and wisdom.

It is a fact that misery wants your company. In Proverbs 27:19 (TLB) we read, *A mirror reflects a man's face, but what he is really like is shown by the kind of friends he chooses.* Proverbs 13:20 tells us, *He that walketh with wise men shall be wise: but a companion of fools shall be destroyed.* We become like those with whom we associate.

Some years ago I found myself at a stagnation point in my life. I was unproductive and unable to see clearly God's direction. One day I noticed that almost all of my friends were in the same situation. When we got together, all we talked about was our problems. As I prayed about this matter, God showed me that He desired that

I have "foundational-level" people in my life. Such people who bring out the best in us, those who influence us to become better people ourselves. They cause us to have greater faith and confidence, to see things from God's perspective. After being with them, our spirits and our sights are raised.

I have found that **it is better to be alone than in the wrong company.** A single conversation with the right person can be more valuable than many years of study.

The Lord showed me that I needed to change my closest associations, and that there were some other people I needed to have contact with on a regular basis. These were men and women of great faith, those who made me a better person just by being around them. They were the ones who saw the gifts in me and could correct me in a constructive, loving way. My choice to change my closest associations was a turning point in my life.

When you surround yourself and affiliate with the right kind of people, you enter into the God-ordained power of agreement. Ecclesiastes 4:9,10,12 (TLB) states:

Two can accomplish more than twice as much as one, for the results can be much better. If one falls, the other pulls him up; but if a man falls when he is alone, he's in trouble.

And one standing alone can be attacked and defeated, but two can stand back-to-back and conquer; three is even better, for a triple-braided cord is not easily broken.

You need to steer clear of negative-thinking "experts." **Remember: in the eyes of average people average is always considered outstanding.** Look carefully at the closest associations in your life, for that is the direction you are heading.

DAY 18

WE ARE CALLED TO STAND OUT, NOT TO BLEND IN

A majority, many times, is a group of highly motivated snails. If a thousand people say something foolish, it's still foolish. Truth is never dependent upon consensus of opinion.

In 1 Peter 2:9, the Bible says of us Christians, ...*ye are a chosen generation, a royal priesthood, an holy nation, a peculiar people; that ye should shew forth the praises of him who hath called you out of darkness into his marvellous light.*

Romans 12:2 exhorts us, *And be not conformed to this world, but be ye transformed by the renewing of your mind, that ye may prove what is that good, and acceptable, and perfect, will of God.*

One of the greatest compliments that anybody can give you is to say that you are different. We Christians live in this world, but we are aliens. We should talk differently, act differently, and perform differently. We are called to stand out.

There should be something different about you. If you don't stand out in a group, if there is not something unique or different in your life, you should re-evaluate yourself.

One way to stand head and shoulders above the crowd is to choose to do regular, ordinary things in an extraordinary and supernatural way with great enthusiasm. God has always done some of His very best work through remnants, when the circumstances appear to be stacked against them. In fact, in every battle described in the Bible, God was always on the side of the "underdog," the minority.

Majority rule is not always right. It is usually those people who don't have dreams or visions of their own who want to take a vote. People in groups tend to agree on courses of action that they as individuals know are not right.

Don't be persuaded or dissuaded by group opinion. It doesn't make any difference whether anyone else believes, you must believe. **Never take direction from a crowd for your personal life. And never choose to quit just because somebody else disagrees with you.** In fact, the two worst things you can say to yourself when you get an idea is: 1) "That has never been done before," and 2) "That has been done before." Just because somebody else has gone a particular way and not succeeded does not mean that you too will fail.

Be a pioneer, catch a few arrows, and stand out.

DAY 19

SAY NO TO MANY GOOD IDEAS

One of the tricks of the devil is to get us to say yes to too many things. Then we end up being spread so thin that we are mediocre in everything and excellent in nothing.

There is one guaranteed formula for failure, and that is to try to please everyone.

There is a difference between something that is good and something that is right. Oftentimes, it is a challenge for many people to discern that which is good from that which is right. As Christians, our higher responsibility is always to do the right things. These come first. We should do the things that we're called to do, the things that are right, with excellence, first — before we start diversifying into other areas.

There comes a time in every person's life when he must learn to say no to many good ideas. In fact, the more an individual grows, the more opportunities he will have to say no. Becoming focused is a key to results.

Perhaps no other virtue is so overlooked as a key to growth and success. The temptation is always to do a little bit of everything.

Saying no to a good idea doesn't always mean never. No may mean not right now.

There is power in the word no. No is an anointed word, one which can break the yoke of overcommitment and weakness. No can be used to turn a situation from bad to good, from wrong to right. Saying no can free you from burdens that you really don't need to carry right now.

It can also allow you to devote the correct amount of attention and effort to God's priorities in your life.

I'm sure that as you read the title of this nugget, past experiences and present situations come to mind. I'm sure you recall many situations in which no or not right now would have been the right answer. Don't put yourself through that kind of disappointment in the future.

Yes and no are the two most important words that you will ever say. These are the two words that determine your destiny in life. How and when you say them affects your entire future.

Saying no to lesser things can mean saying yes to the priorities in your life.

DAY 20

WHEN YOU REFUSE TO CHANGE, YOU END UP IN CHAINS

We humans are custom-built for change.

Inanimate objects like clothes, houses, and buildings don't have the ability to truly change. They grow out of style and become unusable. But at any point in time, at any age, any one of us is able to change. To change doesn't always mean to do the opposite. In fact, most of the time, it means to add on to or slightly adjust.

When we are called upon by the Lord to change, we will continue to reach toward the same goal, but perhaps in a slightly different way. When we refuse to cooperate with the change that God is requiring of us, we make chains that constrain and restrict us.

There are three things that we know about the future: 1) it is not going to be like the past, 2) it is not going to be exactly the way we think it's going to be, and 3) the rate of change will take place faster than we imagine. The Bible indicates that in the end times in which we are now living, changes will come about much quicker than ever before in history.

In 1803 the British created a civil service position in which a man was required to stand on the cliffs of Dover with a spy glass. His job was to be on the lookout for invasion. He was to ring a bell if he saw the army of Napoleon Bonaparte approaching. Now that was all well and good for the time, but that job was not eliminated until 1945! How many spy glasses on the cliffs of Dover are we still holding onto in our lives? **We should choose not to allow "the way we've always done it" to cause us to miss opportunities God is providing for us today.**

Even the most precious of all gems needs to be chiseled and faceted to achieve its best luster. There is nothing that remains so constant as change. Don't end up like concrete, all mixed up and permanently set.

In Isaiah 42:9, the Lord declares: *Behold, the former things are come to pass, and new things do I declare: before they spring forth I tell you of them*. The Bible is a book that tells us how to respond to change ahead of time. You see, I believe that we can decide in advance how we will respond to most situations. When I was coaching basketball many years ago, I used to tell my players that most situations in a game can be prepared for ahead of time. We used to practice different game situations so that when the players got into an actual game situation they would know how to respond. **One of the main reasons the Bible was written was to prepare us ahead of time, to teach us how to respond in advance to many of the situations that we will encounter in life.**

Choose to flow with God's plan. Be sensitive to the new things He is doing. Stay flexible to the Holy Spirit and know that ours is a God who directs, adjusts, moves, and corrects us. He is always working to bring us into perfection.

DAY 21

"AN ARMY OF SHEEP LED BY A LION WOULD DEFEAT AN ARMY OF LIONS LED BY A SHEEP" — OLD ARAB PROVERB

What are the actions and attributes of a leader? What is it that makes him different from others?

1. A leader is always full of praise.

2. A leader learns to use the phrases "thank you"and "please" on his way to the top.

3. A leader is always growing.

4. A leader is possessed with his dreams.

5. A leader launches forth before success is certain.

6. A leader is not afraid of confrontation.

7. A leader talks about his own mistakes before talking about someone else's.

8. A leader is a person of honesty and integrity.

9. A leader has a good name.

10. A leader makes others better.

11. A leader is quick to praise and encourage the smallest amount of improvement.

12. A leader is genuinely interested in others.

13. A leader looks for opportunities to find someone doing something right.

14. A leader takes others up with him.

15. A leader responds to his own failures and acknowledges them before others have to discover and reveal them.

16. A leader never allows murmuring — from himself or others.

17. A leader is specific in what he expects.

18. A leaders holds accountable those who work with him.

19. A leader does what is right rather than what is popular.

20. A leader is a servant.

A leader is a lion, not a sheep.

DAY 22

PEOPLE ARE BORN ORIGINALS,
BUT MOST DIE COPIES

The call in your life is not a copy.

In this day of peer pressure, trends, and fads, we need to realize and accept that each person has been custom-made by God the Creator. Each of us has a unique and personal call upon our lives. We are to be our own selves and not copy other people.

Because I do a lot of work with churches, I come into contact with many different types of people. One time I talked over the phone with a pastor I had never met and who did not know me personally. We came to an agreement that I was to visit his church as a consultant. As we were closing our conversation and were setting a time to meet at the local airport, he asked me, "How will I know you when you get off the plane?"

"Oh, don't worry, pastor; I'll know you," I responded jokingly. "You all look alike."

The point of this humorous story is this: **be the person God has made YOU to be.**

The call of God upon our lives is the provision of God in our lives. We do not need to come up to the standards of anyone else. **The average person compares himself with others, but we Christians should always compare ourselves with the person God has called us to be.** That is our standard — God's unique plan and design for our lives. How the Lord chooses to deal with others has nothing to do with our individual call in life or God's timing and direction for us.

You and I can always find someone richer than we are, poorer than we are, or with more or less ability than we have. But how other people are, what they have, and what happens in their lives, has no effect upon our call. In Galatians 6:4 (TLB) we are admonished: *Let everyone be sure that he is doing his very best, for then he will have the personal satisfaction of work well done, and won't need to compare himself with someone else.*

God made you a certain way. You are unique. You are one of a kind. To copy others is to cheat yourself out of the fullness of what God has called you to be and to do.

So, choose to accept and become the person God has made you to be. Tap into the originality and creative genius of God in your life.

DAY 23

STOP EVERY DAY AND LOOK AT THE SIZE OF GOD

Who is God? What is His personality like? What are His character traits?

According to the Bible, He is everlasting, just, caring, holy, divine, omniscient, omni-potent, omni-present and sovereign. He is light, perfection, abundance, salvation, wisdom, and love. He is the Creator, Savior, Deliverer, Redeemer, Provider, Healer, Advocate, and Friend. Never forget Who lives inside of you: ...*the Lord...the great God, the great King above all gods* (Ps. 95:3 NIV).

John, the beloved disciple, tells us: *Ye are of God, little children, and have overcome them: because greater is he that is in you, than he that is in the world* (1 John 4:4). Period. Exclamation point. That settles it!

God and the devil are not equal, just opposite.

I travel by air quite often and one of the benefits is that every time I fly I get a glimpse of God's perspective. I like looking at my challenges from 37,000 feet in the air. **No problem is too large for God's intervention, and no person is too small for God's attention.**

God is always able. If you don't need miracles, you don't need God. Dave Bordon, a friend of mine, said it best: "I don't understand the situation, but I understand God."

The miraculous realm of God always has to do with multiplication, not addition.

God likens our life in Him to seedtime and harvest. Do you realize how miraculous that is? Let me give you a conservative example: Suppose one kernel of corn produces one stalk with two ears, each ear having 200 kernels. From those 400 kernels come 400 stalks with 160,000 kernels. All from one kernel planted only one season earlier.

Our confession to the Lord should be Jeremiah 32:17 (NIV): *"Ah, Sovereign Lord, you have made the heavens and the earth by your great power and outstretched arm. Nothing is too hard for you."*

God is bigger than_____ _____ . Fill in the blank for your own life.

DAY 24

RETREAT TO ADVANCE

Sometimes the most important and urgent thing we can do is get away to a peaceful and anointed spot.

This is one of the most powerful concepts that I personally have incorporated into my life. I'm sitting right now writing this book in a cabin up on a hill overlooking a beautiful lake, miles away from the nearest city.

As we choose to draw away for a time, we can see and hear much more clearly about how to go ahead. Jesus did this many times during His earthly life, especially just before and after major decisions. The Bible says, *...in quietness and in confidence shall be your strength...*(Is. 30:15). There's something invigorating and renewing about retreating to a quiet place of rest and peace. Silence is an environment in which great ideas are birthed.

There really are times when you should not see people, times when you should direct your whole attention toward God. I believe that every person should have a place of refuge, one out of the normal scope of living, one where he can "retreat to advance" and "focus in" with just the Lord and himself.

It is important to associate intently and as often as possible with your loftiest dreams. In Isaiah 40:31 we read, *But they that wait upon the Lord shall renew their strength; they shall mount up with wings as eagles; they shall run, and not be weary; and they shall walk, and not faint.* Learn to wait upon the Lord.

Make a regular appointment with yourself; it will be one of the most important you can ever have during the course of a week or a month. Choose to retreat to advance. See how much clearer you move forward with God as a result.

DAY 25

HAVE A READY WILL AND WALK,
NOT IDLE TIME AND TALK

Acting on God's will is like riding a bicycle: if you don't go on, you go off!

Once we know God's will and timing, we should be instant to obey, taking action without delay. Delay and hesitation when God is telling us to do something now is sin. The longer we take to act on whatever God wants us to do, the more unclear His directives become. We need to make sure that we are on God's interstate highway and not in a cul-de-sac.

Ours is a God of velocity. He is a God of timing and direction. These two always go together. It is never wise to act upon only one or the other. Jumping at the first opportunity seldom leads to a happy landing. In Proverbs 25:8 the writer tells us, *Go not forth hastily to strive, lest thou know not what to do in the end thereof, when thy neighbour hath put thee to shame.* A famous saying holds that people can be divided into three groups:

1) those who make things happen, 2) those who watch things happen, and 3) those who wonder what's happening. Even the right direction taken at the wrong time is a bad decision.

Most people miss out on God's best in their lives because they're not prepared. The Bible warns us that we should be prepared continually. The Apostle Paul exhorts us: *...be instant in season, out of season...*(2 Tim. 4:2).

There is a seasonality to God. In Ecclesiastes 3:1 we read: *To every thing there is a season, and a time to every purpose under heaven.* Everything that you and I are involved in will have a spring (a time of planting and nurturing), a summer (a time of greatest growth), a fall (a time of harvest), and a winter (a time of decisions and planning).

Relax. Perceive, understand, and accept God's divine timing and direction.

DAY 26

WHEN WISDOM REIGNS,
IT POURS

We should expect wisdom to be given to us. The Bible says in James 1:5, *If any of you lack wisdom, let him ask of God, that giveth to all men liberally, and upbraideth not; and it shall be given him.*

When you have heard God's voice, you have heard His wisdom. Thank God for His powerful wisdom. It forces a passage through the strongest barriers.

Wisdom is seeing everything from God's perspective. It is knowing when and how to use the knowledge that comes from the Lord. The old saying is true, "He who knows nothing, doubts nothing." But it is also true that he who knows has a solid basis for his belief.

Just think, we human beings have available to us the wisdom of the Creator of the universe. Yet **so few drink at the fountain of His wisdom; most just rinse out their mouths.** Many may try to live without the wisdom of the bread of life, but they will die in their efforts.

The world doesn't spend billions of dollars for wisdom. It spends billions in search of wisdom. Yet it is readily available to everyone who seeks its divine source.

There are ten steps to gaining godly wisdom:

1. Fear God (Ps. 111:10)

2. Please God (Eccl. 2:26)

3. Hear God (Prov. 2:6)

4. Look to God (Prov. 3:13)

5. Choose God's way (Prov. 8:10,11)

6. Be humble before God (Prov. 11:2)

7. Take God's advice (Prov. 13:10)

8. Receive God's correction (Prov. 29:15)

9. Pray to God (Eph. 1:17)

10. Know the Son of God (1 Cor. 1:30)

DAY 27

HEARING TELLS YOU THAT THE MUSIC IS PLAYING; LISTENING TELLS YOU WHAT THE SONG IS SAYING

One of the least developed skills among us human beings is that of listening. There are really two different kinds of listening. There is the natural listening in interaction with other people, and there is spiritual listening to the voice of God.

It has been said, "Men are born with two ears, but only one tongue, which indicates that they were meant to listen twice as much as they talk." In natural communication, leaders always "monopolize the listening." **What we learn about another person will always result in a greater reward than what we tell him about ourselves.** We need to learn to listen and observe aggressively. We must try harder to truly listen, and not just to hear.

In regard to spiritual listening, Proverbs 8:34,35 (NIV) quotes wisdom who says:

Blessed is the man who listens to me, watching daily at my doors, waiting at my doorway.

For whoever finds me finds life and receives favor from the Lord.

There is great wisdom and favor to be gained by listening.

Proverbs 15:31 (NIV) says, *He who listens to a life-giving rebuke will be at home among the wise.* Listening allows us to maintain a teachable spirit. It increases our "teach-ability." Those who give us a life-giving rebuke can be a great blessing to us.

The Bible teaches that we are to be quick to listen and slow to speak. (James 1:19.) We must never listen passively, especially to God. If we resist hearing, a hardening can take place in our lives. Callousness can develop. In Luke 16:31 (NIV), Jesus said of a certain group of people, "…'*If they do not listen to Moses and the Prophets, they will not be convinced even if someone rises from the dead.*'" The more we resist listening to the voice of God, the more hardened and less fine-tuned our hearing becomes.

There are results of spiritual hearing, as we see in Luke 8:15 (NIV). This passage relates to the parable of the sower: "…*the seed on good soil stands for those with a noble and good heart, who hear the word, retain it, and by perseveringly produce a crop.*'' Harvest is associated not only with persevering and good seed in good soil, but also with those people who hear the Word of God and retain it.

Fine-tune your natural and spiritual ears to listen and learn.

DAY 28

GOD IS NOT YOUR PROBLEM; GOD IS ON YOUR SIDE

Some time ago I was eating at a Mexican fast food restaurant. As I stood in line for service I noticed in front of me a very poor elderly lady who looked like a street person. When it came her turn, she ordered some water and one taco. As I sat in the booth right next to her, I couldn't help but observe and be moved with compassion toward her. Shortly after I had begun my meal I went over to her and asked if I could buy some more food for her lunch. She looked at me and angrily asked, "Who are you?"

"Just a guy who wants to help you," I responded. She ignored me. I finished my meal about the same time she did, and we both got up to leave. I felt led to give her some money. In the parking lot I approached her and offered her some cash. Her only response to me was, "Stop bothering me." Then, she stormed off.

Immediately, the Lord showed me that this is often the way many of us respond to

Him. When He calls out to us, seeking to bless us, we act as though we don't even know Who He is. We respond to His offer of blessing by asking, "Who are You? What do You want from me?" The Lord, being the gracious God He is, continues to try to bless us. Yet we react by saying, "Stop bothering me." We walk off, just as this lady did, missing out on the rich blessings of the Lord.

It's not the absence of problems that gives us peace; it's God's presence with us in the problems. In Matthew 28:20, Jesus sent His disciples into all the world, ordering them to preach the Gospel to every creature: *Teaching them to observe all things whatsoever I have commanded you; and, lo, I am with you always, even unto the end of the world.* In Romans 8:38,39 (NIV), the Apostle Paul writes, *For I am convinced that neither death nor life, neither angels nor demons, neither the present nor the future, nor any powers, neither height nor depth, nor anything else in all creation, will be able to separate us from the love of God that is in Christ Jesus our Lord.* In verse 31 he declares, *What, then, shall we say in response to this? If God is for us, who can be against us?* A paraphrase might be, "If God is for us, who cares who is against us?"

In Psalm 145:18 (NIV), we read, *The Lord is near to all who call on him, to all who call on him in truth.* James 4:8 (NIV) admonishes us, *Come near to God and he will come near to you.* In Acts 17:27 (NIV) Paul speaks: *"'For in him we live and move and have our being.'"*

Thank God that we can, without hesitation and with full confidence, lean on His eternal faithfulness.

DAY 29

LEARN THE ALPHABET FOR SUCCESS

A Action

B Belief

C Commitment

D Direction

E Enthusiasm

F Faith

G Goals

H Happiness

I Inspiration

J Judgment

K Knowledge

L Love

M Motivation

N Nonconformity

O Obedience

P Persistence

Q   Quality

R   Righteousness

S   Steadfastness

T   Thankfulness

U   Uniqueness

V   Vision

W   Wisdom

X   (E)xcellence

Y   Yieldedness

Z   Zeal

DAY 30

THE MEASURE OF A WOMAN IS NOT WHAT SHE DOES ON SUNDAY, BUT RATHER WHO SHE IS MONDAY THROUGH SATURDAY

You don't have to come out of the Spirit realm. The same closeness, strength, joy, and direction you experience on Sunday, God intends for you to walk in the rest of the week. The devil is waiting to ambush you as you leave church. He wants to bring to your mind thoughts of fear, doubt, unbelief, and destruction.

That's why we believers must guard our minds and hearts. As spiritual creatures, we walk by faith, not by sight. (2 Cor. 5:7.) We are commanded to live in the Spirit and not in the natural.

A person whose eyes, ears, and mind are directed toward the world finds it difficult to hear God speaking to him. The Lord wants to talk to you at work, at lunch, at play — everywhere you go. Some of my greatest revelations from God have come not in my prayer closet, but rather "out of the blue" in the midst of my normal, everyday life.

Our inner man is always willing, but our natural man resists. That's what Jesus meant when He said to His disciples, *Watch and pray, that ye enter not into temptation; the spirit indeed is willing, but the flesh is weak* (Matt. 26:41.)

The advantage of living and walking in the Spirit is that it keeps us on the right path. In Galatians 5:16, 17 (NIV) the Apostle Paul writes: *So I say, live by the Spirit, and you will not gratify the desire of the sinful nature. For the sinful nature desires what is contrary to the Spirit, and the Spirit what is contrary to the sinful nature. They are in conflict with each other, so that you do not do what you want. But if you are led by the Spirit, you are not under law.*

Thank God that our relationship with Him is not a "some-time affair," it's an "all-the-time union." In the words of the old hymn, "He leadeth me! O blessed thought!"

DAY 31

GOD WILL USE YOU RIGHT WHERE YOU ARE TODAY

You don't need to do anything else for God to begin to use you now. You don't have to read another paperback book, listen to another cassette tape, memorize another scripture, plant another seed gift, or repeat another creed or confession. You don't even need to attend another church service before God will begin to make use of you.

God uses willing vessels, not brimming vessels. Throughout the Bible, in order to fulfill His plans for the earth, God used many people from all walks of life. He used:

1. Matthew, a government employee, who became an apostle.

2. Gideon, a common laborer, who became a valiant leader of men.

3. Jacob, a deceiver, whose name became Israel.

4. Deborah, a housewife, who became a judge.

5. Moses, a stutterer, who became a deliverer.

6. Jeremiah, a child, who fearlessly spoke the Word of the Lord.

7. Aaron, a servant, who became God's spokesman.

8. Nicodemus, a Pharisee, who became a defender of the faith.

9. David, a shepherd boy, who became a king.

10. Hosea, a marital failure, who prophesied to save Israel.

11. Joseph, a prisoner, who became prime minister.

12. Esther, an orphan, who became a queen.

13. Elijah, a homely man, who became a mighty prophet.

14. Joshua, an assistant, who became a conqueror.

15. James and John, fishermen, who became close disciples of Christ and were known as "sons of thunder."

16. Abraham, a nomad, who became the father of many nations.

17. Peter, a businessman, who became the rock on which Christ built His Church.

18. Jacob, a refugee, who became the father of the twelve tribes of Israel.

19. John the Baptist, a vagabond, who became the forerunner of Jesus.

20. Mary, an unknown virgin, who gave birth to the Son of God.

21. Nehemiah, a cupbearer, who built the wall of Jerusalem.

22. Shadrach, Meshach, and Abednego, Hebrew exiles, who became great leaders of the nation of Babylon.

23. Hezekiah, a son of an idolatrous father, who became a king renowned for doing right in the sight of the Lord.

24. Isaiah, a man of unclean lips, who prophesied the birth of God's Messiah.

25. Paul, a persecutor, who became the greatest missionary in history and author of two-thirds of the New Testament.

All God needs to use you is all of you!

* * *

A FINAL WORD

Be the whole person God called you to be. Don't settle for anything less. Don't look back. Look forward and decide today to take steps toward His plan for your life.

And remember First Thessalonians 5:24: **Faithful is he that calleth you, who also will do it.**

"Part VI" is adapted from *An Enemy Called Average* (Tulsa: Harrison House, 1990).

WHAT IS YOUR DECISION?

If you have never received Jesus Christ as your personal Lord and Savior, why not do it right now? Simply repeat this prayer with sincerity: "Lord Jesus, I believe that You are the Son of God. I believe that You became man and died on the cross for my sins. I believe that God raised You from the dead and made You the Savior of the world. I confess that I am a sinner and I ask You to forgive me, and to cleanse me of all my sins. I accept Your forgiveness, and I receive You as my Lord and Savior. In Jesus' name, I pray. Amen."

"...if you confess with your mouth, 'Jesus is Lord,' and believe in your heart that God raised him from the dead, you will be saved. For it is with your heart that you believe and are justified, and it is with your mouth that you confess and are saved....for, 'Everyone who calls on the name of the Lord will be saved.'"

Romans 10:9,10,13 NIV

"If we confess our sins, he is faithful and just and will forgive us our sins and purify us from all unrighteousness."

1 John 1:9 NIV

Now that you have accepted Jesus as your Savior:

1. Read your Bible *daily*. It is your spiritual food that will make you a strong Christian.

2. Pray and talk to God daily. He desires for the two of you to communicate and share your lives with each other.

3. Share your faith with others. Be bold to let others know that Jesus loves them.

4. Regularly attend a local church where Jesus is preached, where you can serve Him and where you can fellowship with other believers.

5. Let His love in your heart touch the lives of others by your good works done in His name.

Please let us know of the decision you made. Write:

HONOR
BOOKS

P.O. Box 55388
Tulsa, OK 74155

**Valerie Grant-Soko-losky** is president of VALERIE AND COM-PANY, an international training and consult-ing firm in Dallas, Texas. She is a well-published author of two books, *Corporate Protocol* and *Seasons of Success* and speaks with authority on management and personal development topics. Her client list is a "who's who" of Fortune 500 companies including Texaco, Chemical Bank, Hoechst-Roussel Celanese, Motorola and British Airways. Her credentials in sales/service and communication have led her to be a regular with Nightingale-Conant, the world's largest producers of audio cassette programs, and she hosts radio and television programs.

Quoted often in magazines and newspapers including Southwest Airlines *Spirit Magazine, Dallas Morning News, Washington Post, Meeting Manager* and *Glamour*, Valerie has influenced the corporate world with her consulting and training programs. With humor, wit and well-targeted examples, her speaking engagements define what is expected and respected in today's global business environment...from "The Fine Art of Business Entertaining" to all facets of "Professionalism in the Workplace."

To contact the author regarding seminars, write or call:

Valerie Grant-Sokolosky
Valerie and Company
13140 Coit Road, Suite 516
Dallas, Texas 75240
(214) 644-0444

Additional copies of this book
are available from your local bookstore.

The Topical Bible
Paperback Series

Dare To Succeed — Business Edition
The Mother's Topical Bible
The Father's Topical Bible
The Teen's Topical Bible
The Businessman's Topical Bible
The Businesswoman's Topical Bible
Our Life Together

Available from your local bookstore.

HONOR BOOKS
Tulsa, Oklahoma 74155